6

Classic
PATHFINDER

Patterns and procedures

HEATHER RENDALL

D0995898

CiLT The National Centre for Languages

This compilation first published 2006

by CILT, the National Centre for Languages
20 Bedfordbury
London
WC2N 4LB

This compilation copyright © CILT, the National Centre for Languages 2006

Stimulating grammatical awareness: A fresh look at language acquisition first published by CILT 1998; second edition 2006; © CILT, the National Centre for Languages 2006

Effective MLF grammar teaching first published by Folens 2000; second edition 2006; © CILT, the National Centre for Languages 2006

ISBN 1 904243 42 8

A catalogue record for this book is available from the British Library

Printed in Great Britain by Hobbs the Printer Ltd

CILT Publications are available from: Central Books, 99 Wallis Rd, London E9 5LN. Tel: 0845 458 9910. Fax: 0845 458 9912.

Contents

Acknowledgements

I would like to thank all those teachers and their pupils who, unwittingly or not, have furnished examples used in this book! In particular colleagues via the Lingu@NET Forum, who provided excellent new examples of student errors, and the former Modern Language Department of Tenbury Wells High School, led by Jeanne Atkins, who allowed me access to their pupils for four years.

Above all I thank those 28 people, who as pupils back in 1995–97 formed my research group, who put up with my activities and tests for three years with (apparent) goodwill and (mostly) good humour.

Foreword

Where do our assumptions about how pupils learn a foreign language come from? This is a fundamental question of *Patterns and procedures*, which brings together the main elements of Pathfinder 33: *Stimulating grammatical awareness: A fresh look at language acquisition* (CILT 1998) and *Effective grammar teaching* (Folens 2000), updated to the current context. In this new version, Heather Rendall challenges many of the assumptions about second-language acquisition which have informed our teaching since the arrival of the National Curriculum. She puts her arguments squarely in the context of the recent Key Stage 3 Framework for teaching Modern Foreign Languages and heralds a new era of explicit discussion about language, and especially grammar, in the classroom. However, in order for this discussion to take place, MFL teachers need to understand more about how their pupils make progress and what the word 'grammar' really means.

Many of the assumptions we make about language learning have come from comparing the acquisition of our mother tongue to the learning of a second language. For example the focus on speaking and listening, the tolerance of error and the reduced role of reading and writing in at least the early stages of language learning, which became features of the National Curriculum, are based on studies of mother-tongue acquisition. However, this has commonly led to practice such as insufficient attention to correcting pupils' errors, teaching chunks of language which are not broken down and not showing the pupils the written word. Pupils who are already able to read and write in their mother tongue therefore start to invent their own, often erroneous, systems and patterns, in order to understand the new language. In the first part of the book 'Stimulating grammatical awareness', the author suggests that pupils be enabled to use the linguistic ability they already have in order to achieve a more confident and accurate knowledge of the target language. She describes a series of practical activities firstly to develop the pupils' understanding of sound/spelling relationships, then to support their pronunciation and accuracy through self-correction and finally to help them memorise spellings in the target language. These last areas of memorising and accuracy can be greatly enhanced by the use of ICT, which allows pupils to learn by frequent repetition and correction.

This focus on explicit discussion of language-learning strategies fits in well with the approaches of both the Key Stage 3 and Key Stage 2 Frameworks for teaching MFL. In the second part of the book, 'Active grammar', there is more exploration of how we define the grammar we expect to include in the languages curriculum and how we can move from an implicit to a more explicit approach to teaching it. A simple skill such as using the target-language dictionary can lead to many comical errors in mistranslation unless pupils have an understanding of the grammatical knowledge needed in order to use a dictionary effectively. Again, practical activities are suggested which enable pupils to develop their understanding of grammar per se and to visualise how grammatical structures work in the target language. The author has put to good use research into neuro-linguistics in order to devise the activities and many of her suggestions link to studies of how learning takes place in the brain. She also identifies certain problematic areas, such as teaching gender, word order and reflexive verbs, and includes a range of teaching strategies that can reinforce these concepts and enable pupils to remember and reuse language accurately and with confidence.

Thus, with a more solid linguistic foundation, achieved through the kind of activities and over-arching strategies proposed here by Heather Rendall, pupils can develop more understanding of language learning and so greater creativity and independence.

Ruth Bailey
Language Teaching Adviser, CILT, the National Centre for Languages

Introduction

This book comprises the main elements of two books: Pathfinder 33 *Stimulating grammatical awareness: A fresh look at language acquisition* (CILT 1998) and *Effective MFL grammar teaching* (Folens 2000). In the intervening time (eight and five years respectively) so much has occurred in the field of primary and secondary education that the introductions from both books have been rendered superfluous! There is no longer a need to plead the case, as they did, for including grammar or grammatical awareness in foreign language teaching. The National Literacy Strategy within the primary sector and the MFL KS3 Framework in the secondary sector have placed knowledge of language, an understanding of grammar and the ability to talk about language and grammar, firmly at the heart of teaching. So instead, this compilation can now concentrate on how to put all of these into practice.

This book has two parts:

Part 1: *Stimulating grammatical awareness* takes a lateral look at learning. It looks at the pupils and asks:

- Why is it that some of them seem unable to make use of what we teach them?
- Why do they make the mistakes they do?
- Could their misunderstandings and errors tell us anything about how they approach language learning?
- Can we fathom what they are making of what we are teaching?
- Are there needs that we are not addressing?

Part 2: *Active grammar* then takes a similar, lateral look but at grammar.

- What actually is grammar?
- Why do we need to include it in our teaching?
- Why do pupils need to be introduced not just to grammar but its metalanguage as well?
- Are some mistakes not mistakes but errors? What is the difference?
- Can we predict errors that our pupils are likely to make?
- If certain errors are part of the developing 'feel for the target language', how can we help them accelerate through these predictable behaviours?

Using actual examples of pupil error and pupils' own comments, I explore answers to both sets of questions and then suggest practical ideas for classroom use.

Part 1

Stimulating grammatical awareness

A fresh look at language acquisition

1 Doing what comes naturally

It's a funny thing – language learning. We all seem to do it so easily first time around – so much so that there is a school of thought, which believes that, by researching into a child's acquisition of its mother tongue and applying those 'natural' methods to foreign language learning, they will arrive at some linguistic Philosopher's Stone – a method that will be successful with all.

The reality of most foreign language learning is anything but natural. By force of circumstances it is restricted for most people to a school-based experience. Contact time is often a mere two hours a week; in primary schools it can be as little as 30 minutes a week. There is little or no support in the surrounding social environment. Only a minority of pupils or students have families who can offer help and guidance with homework, let alone supporting learning up to exam level and beyond. And there is no real pressure or motivation in this country, unlike in those of our European neighbours, that drives pupils to learn and then make use of any language once it is learnt.

But even if we could change these negative factors into the most positive set of circumstances possible, there are still two important differences between the natural language learning of a baby/child and the school-based language learning of our pupils that should prevent us from trying to teach using the 'natural method'.

THE NEED FOR A MEANS OF COMMUNICATION

A baby, from birth, communicates using cries and screams or smiles and gurgles. But these are not enough; the child is encouraged ceaselessly by the humans that surround it, to develop and take part in the method of communication called language. This gradually becomes a two way process that, as it evolves, inter alia, makes sense of the infant's surroundings and the events that take place. It is also crucial to the initial process of building up inner thought and all those cognitive procedures that will one day produce reason and judgement, fear and superstition, humour and wit and all those other characteristics of the human psyche.

By contrast, at age eleven, when traditionally the majority of pupils first learn a foreign language, all this is already in place. It is also true, in the main, of Key Stage 2, which is the target for Primary Languages. Pupils have a common means of verbal communication with their teacher and their fellow pupils, which is, in the majority of cases, their mother tongue.

They have a finely developed process of inner thought and are able to understand and make sense of the world around them more or less successfully. The driving forces that power the need for developing a system of communication are absent.

RECOGNISING WORDS

To a baby, language is pure sound. Using a method still not clearly understood, over the first few years of its existence, it is ever more able to differentiate the various and varying elements of sound chains, to identify them with increasing sophistication with meaning and to apply and reapply them both in listening and then speaking.

To most debutant learners of foreign languages, language is more than sound. It is words. From the start of their primary education the emphasis within the curriculum has been on reading and writing. Language has been changed from a pure state to one of artificiality. The two basic language skills of listening and speaking, have been extended to reading and writing. Primary education has by Years 5 and 6 turned pupils into literate beings; they are capable of turning sound into words and words into sound.

So even if we could provide the best of environments for learning a second language – constant contact with the language, motivation for its use, support and encouragement from those around – we still would not have the same natural state of mind in our pupils as a baby has. The literate brain will be seeking all the time to transmute the sound into words that it can store for later recall and use. There is no guarantee that 'natural' methods of learning would now be the best way to learn.

It may prove more fruitful then if, instead, we look at the natural tendencies of first-time second or foreign language learners. During the initial learning period,

- Do learners of second or foreign languages exhibit any distinctive behaviours?
- Can we predict their actions and reactions?
- Can we identify areas of possible confusion and error and act to minimise them?

In brief, is there such a thing as 'natural language learning' a second time around?

Obviously any conclusions drawn here will not be universal. A pupil with good memorisation skills will always outperform a fellow pupil with poor learning skills. A pupil who has extensive experience of another country, another culture, another language, has the advantage over the monolingual person from a narrow background. Pupils, who have the confidence to use new language, will go further than those, who put in little effort.

That having been said, it may still be possible to delineate situations that are common to average pupils beginning their first foreign language lessons and anticipate possible reactions and responses; we just have to bear in mind, when considering our own pupils, that any of these descriptions may fit more or less well and that our pupils' progress through them may be more or less fast and thorough.

Steps in initial language learning

Making sense of a new language

To the average person, any new language is pure babble. No sense can be made of the sounds at all. The sounds are just a continuous stream of noise; the pauses and word/phrase breaks are not immediately discernible and, what is more, it seems to be spoken at a rapid speed. In fact it serves only to reaffirm the worst suspicions of many, that here is something far beyond their grasp – that they are never going to be able to understand, let alone speak this other language.

The one skill that rescues most people is imitation; within days of the start of a holiday abroad, we can manage to pick up and repeat *Grazie*, *Efcharisto*, etc. And it is a truism to state that children are far better at imitating than adults. They do it less self-consciously; they can repeat longer phrases; they can reproduce exact intonation; they can produce between two and six phrases or short sentences held in their heads in short-term memory, even when they don't fully understand the meaning of what they are saying. And they find it fun – mostly! So it is customary for the first foreign language lessons to offer the opportunity to repeat after the teacher a set number of phrases or short sentences; these are usually answers to simple questions referring to personal details such as name, age, address and family. All of this is well within the capability of most pupils and both we and they are pleased (and proud) of the apparent progress being made.

But we should not mistake accurate imitation for progress and understanding. Wholesale copying, both in speaking and in writing, is possible where the general meaning is understood, but the actual value of the individual elements of the language itself can be entirely misunderstood.

How else can errors such as '*je m'appelle grande*' be accounted for? Obviously, the pupil wished to say 'I am big'. She delved into her store of language learnt and experienced, in this case, over two terms in Year 7 and retrieved the phrase '*je m'appelle*' for the meaning of 'I am', as in the sentence 'I am Sarah' = '*Je m'appelle Sarah*'.

The pupil would be capable of making a correct reply both orally and in writing to the question '*Comment t'appelles-tu?*' and so there would be no evidence of her misconception. And yet, however the question had been understood – 'What's your name?' or 'What are you called?' or 'Who are you?', the reply was clearly understood to say 'I'm Sarah'. And the elements of the sentence therefore had to parallel each other in the following manner: 'I'm' + 'Sarah' = '*Je m'appelle*' + '*Sarah*'.

- Have you noticed any such misunderstandings from your pupils? They are more frequently observed in the early stages of learning, but similar misunderstandings can appear for the first time at any stage.
- Do you teach phrases globally?
- Do you transliterate each new phrase for your pupils?

'Chunks' learning

The danger with teaching language globally is that pupils often over-generalise the meaning. Not only do they re-apply the 'chunk' of language inappropriately, as in Sarah's example given above, but they also apply it in an invariable form to cover all related forms of the same meaning. For example: having successfully learnt and practised sentences with '*j'aime*', when they move onto other persons' likes and dislikes, they might re-use the whole sound as if it constituted a single idea – 'like'.

'j'aime le foot' *'papa j'aime' le foot* or even *'papa jem le foot'* = '*papa aime le foot*'

Here are some more examples:

'je m'appelle X' *'Il je m'appelle Pierre'* = Il s'appelle Pierre
'je prends des frites' J'adore *je prends* des frites = J'adore manger des frites

If a verb has been learnt initially in the infinitive, then it is that form that is used to express all manner of meanings:

je aller *mes amis aller* *je suis aller*

It is as if whatever was learnt initially has become an invariable concept, which is so fixed in the mind that pupils find it hard to move onto the next stage of adapting or changing the word according to any grammatical demands.

- Is this a common habit across the ability range?
- Or is it more prevalent among a certain range of pupils?
- If you have recognised it, when would you first expect to see it in the work of your pupils? Very soon? After a term or two? In the second year? Later?
- How long does it take for a pupil to 'get through' this stage?
- Do all pupils successfully 'get through'?

Home-made phonetics

Running in parallel with 'chunks' learning is a tendency to spell by sound, as illustrated in '*papa jem le foot*'. Words or phrases are written phonetically, and, what is more, according to mother-tongue phonics.

An analysis of error in free production of writing reveals a large percentage of misspellings that fall into this category. In Year 7 the number will be high; and the less literate in their mother tongue the pupil, the greater the percentage. Among common examples to be seen are:

'je mappel'	'il sap ell'	'jabbite'	'Ya'	'Nine'	'ik vone'
(je m'appelle)	(il s'appelle)	(j'habite)	(Ja)	(Nein)	(ich wohne)

Some Year 11 pupils are still producing written work along these lines: other pupils seem to be able to avoid doing it from day one.

- What does this evidence tell us about the ways in which pupils are storing and retrieving vocabulary?

- What conclusions can we draw about pupils who show evidence of this kind of home-grown phonetic writing?
- What conclusions can we draw about pupils who show no evidence of it?
- What can we do about it?

Desperately seeking patterns

These are just a few examples of pupil production that you may have encountered. What they reveal are, on the whole, predictable patterns of behaviour, whose origins can be traced. Once the cause is understood, steps can be taken to either minimise their influence or redress the imbalance of comprehension. It is also possible to accelerate pupils past these areas of difficulty by introducing new and necessary patterns of thought or procedures for storage and retrieval and then constantly and consistently practising them until these patterns and procedures become automatic; that is until they become cognitive skills.

The theories I am putting forward here have been drawn up as a result of classroom observations over a number of years, analyses of pupils' work and discussions with pupils. They are based on the chaos theory of physics which states that at first all new experience is chaotic, i.e. has no recognisable pattern and acts randomly! Through random interactions, stable forms emerge. Through trial and error, patterns are established until a successful system is created that suits the environment.

Depending on their prior experience and knowledge, our pupils' initial understanding and reaction to a foreign language will be one of linguistic chaos. Like all listeners to an unknown language, they can make no sense of what they hear. The language is merely a concatenation of sound with no apparent regularities or repetitive elements.

In order to cope, they rely on natural skills of imitation and mimicry, but these skills have limitations. When it comes to understanding the individual elements that go to make up the language, then, like all second and foreign language learners everywhere, pupils will make use of their existing language skills.

> *The learner's knowledge of L1 ... forms a basic resource to which the learner, in the initial stages of learning, can turn in his making use of general language principles.* (Ringbom 1986)

Unfortunately, this does not always produce successful strategies. If what is being taught in the foreign language has no counterpart in the mother tongue, then by turning to their knowledge of their own language, pupils are not going to be helped along useful or even correct lines.

FALSE HYPOTHESES

When teacher Patricia Manning wanted to discover by what method or reasoning her Year 7 and Year 9 pupils allocated gender to French nouns, she set them a test and then interviewed them about how they had tackled the task. Had they made a point of learning the gender of nouns? Had they developed a feel for masculine or feminine words? Had they taught themselves some successful rules-of-thumb?

What she uncovered was disturbing. The Year 7 pupils guessed. They had neither understood the need for learning gender nor had they developed a method for allocating it. It was different for the Year 9 pupils. They had taught themselves some rules of thumb. Unfortunately they were not successful ones – but they were what the pupils had worked out for themselves and so the pupils persisted in using them. Among the reasons they gave for allocating gender were:

words containing many e's or ending in e were ... masculine (!);
words for big, powerful, strong and mobile things were masculine;
words for small, soft, static things were feminine;
words with lots of vowels were feminine;
words with lots of consonants were masculine;
strong sounding words were masculine;
soft sounding words were feminine;

and perhaps most disturbing of all (for teachers at least)

... for words for which one couldn't decide, one used l'. (Manning 1991)

Manning's conclusions were that pupils needed to have their attention brought very explicitly to the importance of learning the correct gender and applying the correct form of articles and she resolved to include much more of this in her work with all ages and abilities (for ideas on teaching gender see Chapter 8). Her research also shows us just how important it is that some time should be spent in discussion with pupils in order to discover what strategies and hypotheses about the language they have developed and whether or not they are a help or a hindrance. We are fortunate now to have the time and opportunity to do just that in the regular plenaries incorporated into our lessons as a result of the MFL KS3 Framework. Right from the start of learning, we can take a few minutes at the end of lessons and ask pupils how they are coping with the most basic of learning – new vocabulary. Three objectives 7W1, 7W6 and 7W7 can be the focus by prompting pupils to talk about how they learn new words, whether it is a successful strategy and discussing openly what is currently causing more of a problem, **sound or spelling**. Many of the concepts to be dealt with in this book, and pupils' reactions to them, make ideal content for plenaries, where teachers and pupils alike can openly discuss problems and difficulties that have to be surmounted and possible methods of resolving them.

Choosing what suits your situation best

The following chapters will look at some of the most important areas of linguistic chaos that an average learner beginning a first foreign language may experience. I will suggest ways in which teachers can stimulate and encourage the development of vital initial learning skills.

For the new and burgeoning area of primary language teaching, what follows must be tempered by individual school experience. Depending on when foreign languages are to be introduced, suggestions given here may or may not be pertinent. It has already been suggested that most pupils are literate by the time they begin their MFL studies. So if your school introduces MFL learning in Years 5 and 6, then the following ideas will be of use. However, if your feeder primary schools have decided to introduce languages to the early

Years, before reading and writing in the mother tongue are established, it stands to reason that foreign language teaching cannot be based on those two skills and must be restricted to the two natural skills of listening and speaking. In this case some of the following ideas may not be suitable.

Even if you have 'literate' pupils, not everything that follows may apply to the particular pupils you teach. Like other methodologies, they will be more or less applicable depending on the abilities and learning skills your pupils bring with them into the classroom.

So, for example, if your pupils have been brought up in their primary education to learn yards of poetry by heart, then they will be more capable of learning-homeworks, i.e. learning words and phrases by heart, than pupils who have never been asked to learn anything by heart in their lives. The former will know how to set about it; they will know that they can do it – with a bit of hard work; they will know what it takes and how long it takes.

The latter won't have a clue. They won't know where to start; they may be convinced that this is beyond them; they may not realise how long they have to keep at it. They may not understand that repetition is the key to memorising; they may think that if they cannot remember the first time of looking, that they are already a failure. Convinced of their own inadequacies, they may give up far too soon and so unfortunately confirm their own worst fears. They may need constant help in devising successful learning strategies.

I am not suggesting that all the pupil behaviours described here will be seen in all schools and classes. Some of the situations you may recognise only too well. Others you may never have come across. They are, however, all genuine examples. In reading through the following chapters, you will need constantly to compare what is being described to your own situation. If the evidence of your own experience is mirrored in any of the examples, then the ideas given may be of some help.

Some of the statements made, some of the conclusions drawn contradict current practice and methodological theory. Again, you will have to decide for yourself which theory or theories the evidence of your own experience supports.

2   The seeing ear

Of all the four language skills – reading, writing, listening and speaking – listening is first and foremost. It is possible to learn a language – even a first language – with this skill alone: children unable to verbalise because of physical impairment are still able to learn, understand and respond to language. So listening is the first focus of our attention.

As I pointed out in the previous chapter, our Year 5 or Year 7 pupils no longer have exclusively natural listening skills. They have been educated to 'see' what they hear; to understand that all sound can be translated into words. They are, in this sense, literate. The speed at which we follow speech and make sense of it, under natural circumstances, using our mother tongue, is miraculously fast. We do not need to consciously see the words in our mind's eye. But we can hear where they are, we can separate them and their meanings in order to make sense of what we hear and we can do this so well that, if need be, we can write down what we hear – more or less accurately. None of these skills are immediately available in the target language to the learner of a foreign language. They have to be re-learnt.

One of the major battle grounds of primary education in any mother tongue is the development of accurate orthography: a battle fought between accepted spelling and 'heard' words. An English child who writes 'receeved', 'gimme', 'wassat' or 'hospittle' is not retrieving spellings that have been seen: rather they are his or her own creation. Had the words or phrases been spoken rather than written, no inaccuracy would have been noticeable, as the primitive phonics succeed in reproducing more or less the correct sound. It is only in written work that the homespun phonetics will be apparent and will be marked down as misspellings. 'Receeved' and 'hospittle' are 'heard' words. 'Gimme' and 'wassat' are 'heard' phrases.

What causes a child to misspell, that is to store and retrieve according to its own phonetics? Two possible situations:

- The child does not have sight of the correct spelling often enough. Their experience of the language is in the main aural/oral rather than based on all four skills.
- When mistakes do become apparent, i.e. the words **are** written down, the misspellings are tolerated and not drawn to the child's attention, so no corrections are ever made.

But what can also be deduced from such evidence is that a child can and does store sounds that he or she hears and, if the correct spelling is unknown, retrieves them for writing using an individually devised spelling system. The system so created may be obvious and therefore interpretable by all, e.g. 'Wright a senten to a pen-firend' ('Write a sentence to a pen-friend' or possibly 'Write eight sentences to a pen-friend') or it can be so eccentric as to defy outside interpretation, e.g. 'I no binna colla savage'. (The result of an eight year-old being asked to use the word 'savage' in a sentence. Her intentions have never been satisfactorily explained!). The system may be imperfect even within itself, e.g. a Year 10 boy's French comprehension answers in English included not just 'shert' but also 'shurt' for 'shirt'.

Pupils, hearing a foreign language for the first time, are likely to employ this same skill to make sense of the stream of sound being experienced, even though they may not, as yet, be able to separate it into individual words and phrases. If asked to reproduce either orally or in writing any of the sounds, they will have to retrieve them from memory. They may have stored them aurally (by sound) or graphemically (by letters/phonics). Which ever means has been used, pupils will decode what has been stored using the phonic system they are used to. This could be correct English phonics or it could be an individual system. In speaking, except for the probably heavy accent, the recall should produce a correct response. In writing however we can expect such spellings as:

Wee	J'mapple	Shebeet	Jai abet	saprairde	j'e noe na pai
(Oui)	(Je m'appelle)	(J'habite)	(J'habite)	(c'est près de)	(je n'en ai pas)

Mistakes like this are evidence that our pupils are storing by sound, which they then interpret into written form using their own homespun English phonetics. The reasons for doing this will be similar to those given for the mother tongue. There has been:
• not enough sight of the words themselves;
• not enough correction to change the stored image or interpretation of sound.

How do we avoid this? The answer lies fortunately in the MFL KS3 Framework which has dared to overturn two decades of National Curriculum Non-Statutory Guidance.

Back in 1992 the MFL National Curriculum proposals *Modern Foreign Languages for ages 11–16* stated:

> *In the early stages of learning, the written form of a foreign language can interfere strongly with pronunciation, especially where the script is already familiar. To combat this, learners need ample opportunities to listen and respond before the written forms are involved.*
>
> *Modern Foreign Languages for ages 11–16: 55, 9.6*

Although I can sympathise with the argument about pronunciation, I cannot agree with the conclusion that the solution should be to withdraw the sight of the word. Rather than cure one problem, I believe it may cause another even greater one.

If pupils are being asked to store sound without having ever seen the phonic system by which it is conventionally written, i.e. its correct target-language spelling, then it should come as no surprise to us that they will store it according to their mother-tongue system. While only oral work is required this system may appear to work well. Errors in storage will only become apparent when the words are written down.

If words or phrases are inaccurately stored, there is no chance at all of them being retrieved accurately. Even worse, there is some evidence to show that language stored inaccurately early on is only re-learnt correctly with a great deal of effort on behalf of both pupil and teacher. Without that effort, the original storage/retrieval fossilises. Year 11 students will have had plenty of opportunity over five years to have corrected for themselves or to have had corrected by their teachers that most basic of responses: '*Je m'appelle ...*' but '*je mapple*' or '*jur mapple*' or '*je 'ma pella',* etc still occur as late as GCSE exams.

In order to be able to recognise a sound and associate it with meaning in one's mind, a system of recall has to be built up. Some people depend more on aural recall than visual graphemic recall: that is they recall by hearing the words inside their head rather than seeing the words spelt out. Some people are entirely graphemic: they see words clearly printed in their mind's eye. Others use a mixture of both. In order that all pupils should have the opportunity to build up their own personal recall systems, they need the stimulus of both the sound and the sight of the word.

So my first recommendation is: Every word has three attributes: a meaning, a sound and a spelling. Target language nouns will also have a gender. All four attributes should be presented immediately and simultaneously and repeatedly.

Practice for the ears and eyes

When introducing new words in class, show the written words on separate flashcard labels; these can then be used to play games with the new words.

Matching labels to pictures

Divide the class into two teams: hand out flashcards to one half and word labels to the other half. The group with the flashcards have to hold them up one at a time and the other group have to find the flashcard that matches their label. The first group has to check that the labels are correct. While this activity is going on, you, the teacher, should be calling out the new words. (*matching printed word to meaning: checking pronunciation*)

Matching labels to sound I

Use the same labels: hand out a label to each pupil; depending on the number of words, you may need to have more than one copy of the labels. As you say the word or phrase and hold up the flashcard picture, the pupil or pupils holding that label have to hold it up. (*matching printed word to sound and meaning*)

Extra: Gradually couch words and phrases in phrases and sentences respectively so that the ear is being trained to listen out for and recognise certain specific sounds, for which the pupil has a written prompt. You can also, as vocabulary increases, hand out more than one label to each pupil.

Matching meaning and labels to sound I

Divide the class into two: hand out the flashcards to one group and the labels to the other. Call out the words in the target language. The two pupils in opposing teams who have the picture and the label respectively hold them up high. Which team gets there first? (*matching sound to meaning; matching sound to printed word*)

Matching meaning and labels to sound 2

Divide the class into two: hand out the flashcards to one group and the labels to the other. Call the words out in English. The pupil with the correct flashcards has to call out the target-language word: the other team's member has to hold up the right label. Who gets there first this time? *(matching meaning to printed word; producing sound for meaning)*

Matching labels to sound 2

Divide the class into three groups. Hand out the flashcards to one group, the labels to another. The group with the flashcards holds them up one at a time and the other group has to hold up the matching label: the third group has to say the word aloud. *(matching printed word to meaning; matching sound to printed word and meaning)*

Listening out for words

Create a short story in which the words/phrases being learnt appear and re-appear frequently. Hand out the new words on individual labels. Ask pupils to listen for the word on their label. When they hear it, they have to stand up. When they hear it again, they sit down. A third time and they stand up again and so on. Once the story has been read through once, read it through again and again, only faster! *(matching a written word with a heard sound)*

Try it again without handing out labels. Can the pupils recognise all the words they have just learnt?) Ask them to put a hand up when they recognise a new word and down again when they hear the next. *(matching a word held internally with a heard sound)*

Extra: In low ability classes instead of handing out a list of words to learn to the whole class, make each child or a group of children responsible for learning one word or phrase on behalf of the class. That child or group then becomes the 'class expert' on that word – its meaning, its sound, its spelling and its gender. Pupils should be encouraged to refer to the 'class experts' for help – unless of course they find that they have remembered other people's words as well as their own.

 ## PROGRESSION

From recognising one word labels, move on to devise exercises like these:

1. 'Listen and order' exercise

Aim: to pick out and number words in the order heard.

• Print out a list of vocabulary on small pieces of paper – one for each pupil. You can produce twelve lists like this on one sheet of A4. Hand out a list to each pupil and then call out one word at a time in a different order, making sure you mark down on your own list the order in which you say them!

Mathe
Deutsch
Englisch
Kunst
Religion
Musik
Sport
Informatik

- Pupils have to number the words as they hear them – in this instance 1–8.
- At the end choose a pupil to be a checker, to read back the words aloud in the order given.
- Repeat the whole exercise two or three times, reordering the words each time.
- Whenever there is a natural break in the lesson, in between exercises, ask the pupils to pick up the lists again and read the words aloud again, always using a different order.
- Once it is clear pupils are becoming adept, appoint a pupil to read a new list aloud.

You can ring the changes halfway through the lesson by reading out the English meanings instead. The checker however still gives the answers in the target language.

To start with, you may be surprised at the number of pupils who have difficulty in locating the correct printed word from a list of six to eight words. You may have to say the words very slowly indeed and repeat each one more than once. Even then less able pupils will take an inordinate amount of time spotting the correct word, especially if there are a couple of words with similar spellings, e.g. *chaussettes/chaussures/chemise*. One teacher, into whose lesson I introduced this exercise, was shocked to discover the number of pupils, who were having difficulty. She commented 'No wonder some of them can't find their way round a page of the coursebook. I must sound so fast to them. They can have no idea what words to look for, to match what I'm saying.'

The inability to process sound and match it against letter combinations would seem, from recent research, to lie at the root of many dyslexic problems. The retraining of the ear to correlate sound and spelling has proved very successful in raising children's reading ages. **We are having to re-train all our pupils in a like manner to target language phonics, otherwise they will remain 'dyslexic' in the target language.**

2. Listen and select exercise

Aim: to pick certain words out from a selection of similar looking words or phrases.

- On small sheets of paper print out half a dozen rows of words, each horizontal row having similar sounding words which include the vocabulary being learnt and some unknown words.

bouton	bouteille	au bout	bouche	boue	bouge
chaise	chère	choix	chef	chaîne	
tente	trente	train	tant	tranche	

für	fahren	führen	vor	fürchten	
Weise	wieder	weiden	Wiese	weilen	
Apfel	Bruder	drücken	Äpfel	Druck	Brüder

caballo	cobayo	conejo	cangrejo		
perro	pero	pera	pila	para	
quince	cinco	seis	siete	cuatro	cuarto

Pupils have to circle or underline the word or words you call out.

- Starting with the first row, call out the known words, one word at a time: pupils have to number the words in the order they hear them.
- Check as you go row by row by getting the pupils to call out the words heard.

Extra: As pupils start to get a feel for the target-language phonic system, you can do exercises like these two with words the pupils have not yet seen. This is a real test of their ability to match sound to the printed word. When your pupils are able to achieve tests like this with little effort, you know you will have arrived at the point where you can begin to relax. You know that they can now process sound in the target language and 'see' it in their mind's eye, They are also at a stage where they are likely to be storing correctly and so can move on to the next stage of retrieving correctly. They won't be perfect yet – but at least they are on their way.

3. Listen, read and select

Aim: to listen and pick out the correct spelling from a choice of two.

- Make a set of labels with wrong spellings! Pair them with the label with the correct spelling.
- Hold up a pair of labels and call out the target-language word.
- Pupils have to point to the correct spelling.

There has been a school of thought for many years that prides itself on never showing mistakes to pupils. Such an exercise would be an anathema to them. I actually think it's very useful. I believe from my experience and observations when watching pupils doing such exercises, that they actually accelerate learning. The brain has to come to a decision 'Which one is correct? The one on the left? The one on the right?'

It can only either:

a Know the right answer immediately – because there is an instantaneous check with the correct word lodged in the memory.
b Guess the right answer – because, though knowledge of the meaning and the sound may be solid, the accuracy of the spelling is less certain or non-existent. This can be the case particularly for those pupils who use aural storage for language and whose memorisation techniques of spelling are poor even in their mother tongue.
c Not know the answer at all and wait to follow the rest of the class.

In the last two circumstances, the immediate giving of the correct answer gives the brain a new opportunity to take in the look of the correct spelling. If the exercise is repeated frequently and in short order, these pupils will be helped to build up a store of correct spellings matched to their sounds.

Cognitively speaking, the ability to spot a correct spelling without hesitation can only mean that somewhere inside the brain what is being read outside is being checked inside and matched and found to be OK.

4. Listen and point

Aim: to pinpoint words and phrases in texts and coursebooks.

• Ask pupils to open the coursebook at the double spread about to be tackled.
• Call out whole sentences.
• Pupils make an obvious show of pointing to the right passage.
• Then reduce the content down to phrases and ask pupils to locate them.
• Then reduce down to single words. Can they locate them as well?

To start with you may find few pupils, who can do this competently, but as the class builds up its ability to transform sound heard into words to be read, they will get better and better. An essential activity that should prepare them well for being able to locate any exercise or activity in the coursebook.

Exercises like these should be used first of all as full classroom activities and then re-used as starter activities and should always precede any productive work. If we do not 'fix' the sound of new words in our pupils' brains before we ask them to say them, then all we can expect is immediate imitation. This is transitory. They will have difficulty in producing the same sound a few minutes or lessons later by themselves and will have to rely on our prompting them.

SAYING WHAT WE SEE

However important imitation and repetition are as learning tools, they should not be confused with real speaking production. That will only come much later. National Curriculum Attainment Target levels should not be used to assess reinforcement activities such as these. All learning of vocabulary takes students of any age and level of competence back to Level 1 – single word recognition through to Level 4 – apply new phrases with approximate spelling or pronunciation. Assessment should only be used to judge how far pupils have come by the end of a unit of work or over a period of time. It is a waste of teacher time to assess repetitive reinforcement activities.

It is important that pupils should be encouraged to imitate and repeat silently but aloud inside their heads, i.e. to sub-vocalise, the sound of new words. This is an important step towards internal recall and later on to thinking, and yet few exercises ever ask this of pupils. When I have suggested it, some pupils have appeared surprised, even shocked, that they should be asked to 'think' in the target language!

Pupils will not be able to **produce** the sound of any word **independently**, unless that sound is well and truly lodged in their head. Once pupils can 'hear' the word inside their heads, they will try and say it. Even then they might have difficulty in actually forming the sounds. Some pupils are quite happy to 'have a go'. They don't mind being corrected and will repeat words happily to themselves until they get it right. Others are not so self-assured. They prefer to wait until they feel more certain about being able to say the word correctly. Known as the 'silent period', it is an important step even in first language learning. It is as if the brain needed time to sort out the sound for itself before production. So we should not be insisting that all children speak/imitate simultaneously and immediately and out loud. Rather allow imitation and repetition to be voluntary, as they feel confident. If pupils remain silent they may well be saying it to themselves. Encourage this as a first step.

This is the 'golden rule' in the Primary Immersion Scheme in Canada. The teachers use French all the time, but Year 1 pupils are allowed to use whichever language they like. As their understanding and competence grows, so does their confidence and they move almost unconsciously into the target language.

Some pupils will rush at imitation and repetition. Others will wait on the sidelines. Both attitudes should be tolerated. How many slow starters in first language learning catch up with their prattling peers? A silent child can suddenly burst out into sentences. What is certain is that when a child can do something, he or she will. If a child doesn't feel sure about it, he or she will hesitate and keep silent. Forcing performance may only serve to discourage.

So my second main recommendation is encourage pupils to imitate and repeat either out loud or in their heads. Don't force them to speak but tell them to do so as soon as they feel confident.

MAKING THE BEST USE OF STARTERS

Pupils come into our lessons with English ringing in their ears and minds. Professor Eric Hawkins dubbed foreign language teaching 'Gardening in the gale of English' (Hawkins 1981).

Now that lessons have starter activities, we can make full use of these repetitive five minute slots to present and practise and re-present and re-practise the skills needed to implant a new phonic system into our pupils' ears, as well as 'warming up' our pupils brains. The idea behind a starter/warm-up is rooted in solid psychological fact. The whole of advertising depends on it! If you are reminded of something, that part of your brain is activated: if you see it soon afterwards, you recognise it as being familiar or 'just thought of' and you are more likely to use it, choose it or think about it. If we 'bathe' our pupils in the target language in the first few minutes of every lesson, we will wake up those parts of the brain dealing with the new language: pupils will be made ready for what is to come. **So it is essential that starters should be receptive activities and not productive.** Receptive activities include:

- sound/sight recognition;
- matching meaning.

Later on when the new phonic system has been fixed, activities can develop into:

- accurately writing down from a sound prompt:
- accurate recall from a picture prompt.

An excellent activity for halfway through a unit, which combines listening, reading and speaking and which makes a good starter is aural dominoes.

Aural dominoes

Why these work, I'm not sure. But they do. I have used them for both practising new words and revising old vocabulary from Year 7 to Year 11, using English paired with the target language or a picture paired with the target language. I have even used them to practise GCSE oral questions and specimen answers using only the target language.

The dominoes can be made on an ordinary word processor or DTP using TABLES. The finished products should look like these.

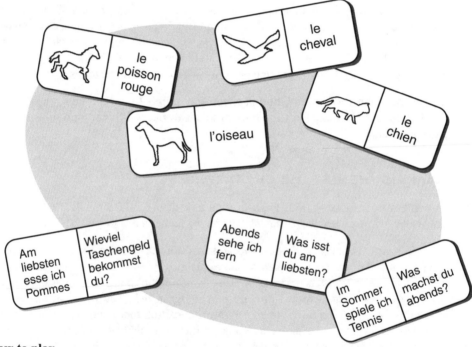

How to play

- You will need one domino per pupil in the class. Any absentees' cards have to be either held by the teacher – which can make life quite busy! – or handed as extras to pupils, especially those you want to keep on their toes.
- Hand out the dominoes making sure that they are going out in random order.
- Then point to any pupil and ask them to call out the word/s in the target language, e.g. '*Le chien!*'

- The pupil who has the domino with either the English word 'dog' or the picture of the dog, stands up and calls out 'dog!' and then says their own target-language word '*L'oiseau!*'.
- The pupil with the word or picture of a bird, stands up and calls out 'bird!' and then reads out their own target-language word '*Le cheval*'.
- Continue like this round the class until all words have been called.
- Repeat but this time keep a check on the time it takes to complete the round of vocabulary.
- Repeat once more but encourage them to try and beat their own record of X minutes.
- By the third go any pupil daydreaming, not listening, not coming up with their response quickly enough for the likings of their fellow pupils will either be pre-empted and have their answer called out by the others or be nudged into answering by neighbours.
- Have another couple of goes at the end of the lesson, each time trying to lower the time it takes to complete the round.

In the next lesson reverse the process and have the English called out first and see if that speeds up the process.

I believe the benefit of this exercise lies somewhere in the practice it gives both ears and eyes. Having the answer in front of you, allows you to anticipate the question. Even if you don't know how to say the target-language word exactly, you stand a good chance of recognising it when someone else says it.

I tried out the GCSE oral question dominoes on a teacher who was herself learning German. She said that it became very easy to hear the word in the question which matched the visual content of her answer.

'*Was machst du abends?*'	'*Abends sehe ich fern.*'
'*Was ißt du am liebsten?*'	'*Am liebsten esse ich Pommes.*'
'*Was für Musik hörst du am liebsten?*'	'*Am liebsten höre ich Popmusik.*'
'*Um wieviel Uhr stehst du auf?*'	'*Ich stehe um sieben Uhr auf.*'

The same cards can be used in extension work by groups. We've found that pupils can have up to six cards each to look at and still be able to respond quickly to questions heard. So a group of five pupils round a table could make use of about 30 dominoes to practise quick-fire questions and answers.

Two side benefits of this exercise are the opportunity it gives teachers to help pupils with pronunciation and the frequency with which all the new words are heard within a short space of time. Fellow pupils are not as tolerant as teachers of poor pronunciation and if there is a break in the chain of rapid fire answers because someone has not said the target-language prompt word clearly enough to be understood, then a barrage of correction will be fired by the rest of the class. Far from being discouraging, results would appear to point to the fact that peer judgement is very motivating indeed.

USING RESOURCE MATERIAL

No language course would be complete without tapes or nowadays CDs and the exercises they offer. But bearing in mind all that has already been suggested about the linguistic chaos of the initial learner's mind and the lack of skills in being able to interpret such vital things as word breaks, phrases and the use of intonation, one has to ask how useful disembodied sound is at the **beginning** of any topic when the new words and structures are still being introduced. At least with video there are all the visual contexts and clues that help in understanding ordinarily what is being said. But a tape is just a stream of sound once again – without the benefit of gesture, facial expression or background.

My third main recommendation is therefore – and it is one already followed by some course books – that pupils look at the tapescript or text as they listen so that they can follow the sound by simultaneously reading.

And the tape should not just be played through once. Pupils should be given the opportunity to listen and read and re-listen and re-read until they are able to close their eyes, listen and 'see' the words running past in their minds eye; until the tape can be stopped at any point, the text turned to and the place located.

If no text exists in the course book, then it is worth every effort it takes to copy it up on a single OHT. Use one pupil at each run-through to stand by the OHP and point to the words as they are heard.

How often you will have to play a single tape exercise until your pupils can follow the words, will depend on them. Do not take it for granted that all pupils can do this straight away. You will need to experiment. Some pupils have 'good ears', others do not.

One way of checking how much has been gained is to follow a listening exercise like this with the flash card label exercise mentioned at the beginning of this chapter. For the final play of the tape, remove the text from sight, hand out word cards to the pupils and see whether and how quickly they can identify their word with the sound by holding up the word card as and when they hear the word.

MAKING OPPORTUNITIES

Although the emphasis in this book is on the initial learning stages when existing skills are being re-developed and new skills gradually built up, I cannot repeat often enough that it takes a long time to establish new skills and an even longer time before they become automatic and can be used without conscious effort. To this end exercises and opportunities to practise the same skills have to continue on a regular basis throughout the learning period.

I have recommended regular aural warm-up exercises used as starters at the beginning of lessons and will make other suggestions in later chapters. Teachers should be looking to have a battery of prepared exercises that they can turn to – almost at a moment's notice – either to fill in the odd two or three minutes at the end of an exercise or to practise something in particular they have noticed as a common error.

3 The listening eye

It is as important to train the eye to 'hear' words when read, as it is to 'see' words when heard. Both of these skills stem from activities that are not natural but learnt. A toddler cannot visualise words because he or she does not know they exist. He or she cannot make sense of the black 'squiggles' in his or her favourite bedtime book, because as yet they do not know how to connect the correct sound to each word and so read them.

So, as you re-train the pupils' ears to 'see' words inside their heads, you also need to be re-training the eye to 'hear' them when they are being read. If we don't, we may well be impeding the progress of our pupils.

In class we obviously use those learning techniques that we believe to be effective – otherwise we wouldn't use them. However the most surprising, unforeseen pitfalls can be revealed in discussions with pupils. One Year 8 boy who was causing constant disruption in a class, explained his behaviour in this way.

Me:	Why do you muck around so much in class?
Him:	I don't like French.
Me:	Why not?
Him:	Cos it's hard.
Me:	Why's it hard?
Him:	Cos you've got to learn lots of words.
Me:	What's hard about learning lots of words?
Him:	They don't sound the same when I get them home.

All I could do was totally agree with him! Why should a pupil who has only a rudimentary feeling for the sound of this new language, be able to carry home with him the correct sound for a dozen or so words?

And yet we hand out lists of words or ask pupils to copy them down into backs of books or vocabulary books in order to 'learn' them at home. I wonder how many pupils in Year 5 or Year 7, when doing this kind of homework, **can** actually hear the correct target-language sound of the words they are learning.

It may be that we have hit on yet another possible reason why the sight of the written word in the target language is thought to have such an effect on children's pronunciation. Could it be because, when they learn them, they are saying the words to themselves using English sounds? Because we have asked them to commit vocabulary to memory before we have satisfactorily fixed target-language sound in their minds? They learn badly because we ask them to learn by heart too soon.

So my first recommendation in this chapter is: let them take the sound home with them.

 ## LEARNING VOCABULARY

If pupils are made to learn vocabulary by heart before they have established good aural recall, then it will not come as a surprise to hear the words being spoken in an English accent. We should never give them this homework unless we can ensure that we send both the sound and sight home with them. This was of course the solution to the Year 8 boy's problem given above. The teacher recorded all the vocabulary to be learnt on to a short tape and the boy was put in charge of the departmental dubbing machine. Any pupil could bring in a tape and he would copy the vocabulary on to it. No one in future needed to go home without the sight and sound of words to be learnt.

If this facility is not available to you, try making use of their natural tendency, i.e. to use their own mother-tongue phonics and, importantly, taking them past it. That is, allow them to write down the sound of the target language in English phonics but make them write it in such as way that they know this is **not** the right spelling. I have always allowed pupils to write their own phonic spelling in brackets underneath new words to be learnt.

Je m'appelle	*J'ai onze ans.*	*Wieviel Uhr ist es?*	*Es ist halb vier.*
(jer ma pell)	(jay onz on)	(vee feel ur ist es?)	(Es ist halp fear)

This is very different from pupils using English phonics to sound new words and should not be confused:

Je m'appelle.	*J'ai onze ans.*	*Wieviel Uhr ist es?*	*Es ist halb vier.*
'Gee ma pelly'	'ge ay onz ans'	'weeveal oor ist ess?'	'Ess ist halb vyer'

I also tell them that they will only be allowed to do this in their first two years of learning, that by the end of that time they should have developed a good enough understanding of the target-language phonic system to be able to write down new words and sound them correctly immediately. I add for good measure that if they can dispense with the English phonics before then, then they will be making excellent progress. This latter comment is enough to make sure that the brighter and more competitive pupils will try to do without English phonics as soon as they can! Weaker, less confident pupils, on the other hand, will have been given a long safety net, long enough for most of them to feel proud when they find themselves capable of dispensing with the English well before the end of their second year of learning.

If this idea appals you, take a look at the successful Usborne Language Guides: it is precisely this method they use to help beginners make use of the phrase book. They are going to use it anyway, so make use of that fact and then give them a deadline for doing without it.

JUST A STRING OF LETTERS?

If we do ask pupils to read or refer to the printed word independently before they can hear the words ringing in their ears, then we should expect that they will develop an 'incompetency' rather than a competency. They will read the target language aloud in the same way as they read their own language. Or worse. They could do what some of us do when we meet not easily pronounceable foreign words … read them silently. That is – we gloss over them.

I call it Russian Name syndrome. Unless we have a knowledge of Russian or the name itself is well known or easy to pronounce (Olga, Ivan, Boris), then we will tend to recognise them as a string of letters, a set spelling: Vorotyntsev, Smyslovsky, Nechvobdov. However often we might see them, we may still have difficulty saying them aloud or remembering them well enough to write them down unaided once away from the book. Some of us may try to say the words; most of us will recognise them as a recurring set of letters without sound and pass over quickly.

If you have ever toured in Wales and have not the slightest idea about Welsh pronunciation, you will have almost certainly experienced the same situation there. How would you say the following to yourself if you met them for the first time in a brochure or on a map: Penrhyndeudraeth or Llanfairynghornwy or Machynlleth. And if you were giving directions to these places, what would you say to your driver?

We need to make absolutely sure that our pupils are developing an awareness of target-language phonics and that this is encouraged, developed and tested by constant reading aloud. We should continue this as an integral part of learning until they reach the stage where they can read independently and accurately – unaided and unprompted by us.

TAKING IT STEP BY STEP

If, as suggested in the previous chapter, you are supporting the sound of the new language with the sight of the new words, then it should follow that the next step is to see how much has been taken on board and whether the sight of the words can now recall their sound.

If you have been doing listening exercises with either written labels or a short text and your pupils have been able to locate the words you say with ease, you can be justifiably confident that the sound and sight of those words are successfully fixed in their mind's eye.

But can they now produce the sound of the word from sight? Like many retrieval processes from the brain, it is not an all-or-nothing situation. It is a skill that will develop gradually in most pupils. The National Curriculum MFL level descriptions map out clearly the progressive steps anticipated between levels 1–4 in learning to say words.

Level 1: they need a spoken prompt – they are still at imitation stage; they have not yet developed the 'internal' sound recall.

Level 2: they are hesitant but having a 'go' – they have moved on but are still not yet at that stage where they can confidently reproduce sound on their own.

Level 3: they can speak independently – but the pronunciation may be approximate.

Level 4: they are speaking independently and in the main accurately but not yet fluently.

This ability to read words aloud is a vital stage in the initial language learning process. We have to make sure, before we 'push on' with our planned course, that our pupils are capable of this, that they really can produce the correct sounds for words – unaided.

If we don't, if we continue regardless, our pupils will find progress harder and harder to achieve. If they are learning words without the correct sound attached, then either they are learning them visually and silently – as a string of letters – or they are saying them as if they were English words. Either way, when they are listening to the target language, they will not recognise in the sounds they hear the word they are supposed to have learnt, nor when they are trying to speak will they be able to conjure up the right pronunciation.

 ## CHECKING PROGRESS

Starters give you an ideal opportunity to keep track of pupils' progress in independent speaking.

Start the lesson by handing out a set of aural dominoes (see page 22) and play a round. Collect in the dominoes, shuffle and re-distribute. Play another round. Repeat for a third time. If no pupil stumbles over or mispronounces any of the words or phrases they have to read, then you have evidence enough that your pupils can match sound to the sight of the written word successfully and have obviously developed a good internal 'ear'.

If they are still reading them *à l'anglaise*, however, or find it impossible to say words without a prompt from you, then it is obvious they still have some way to go. What is more, they are still not at the stage where they can be left to learn words or phrases correctly for themselves.

There is another good reason for doing this at the beginning of the lesson. If they are capable of reading aloud unaided at the beginning of a lesson, when they haven't had a chance yet to warm up their ears and eyes to the target language, then they must be really competent.

STEPS TOWARDS SPEAKING

Of course there will be a grey area as in any process of learning. The sound can be heard in the head, but the confidence to try and reproduce it is lacking. Just a nudge in the right direction is often enough to boost performance. If some pupils' reading is a bit hesitant or not up to their normal standard, then return to the dominoes after doing ten or twenty minutes work. Has the aural input during that time done anything to shake up and re-focus their ability to reproduce sound? The answer will be hopefully: Yes.

When pupils are reading aloud and if they make mistakes, **don't** give them the correct sound to imitate immediately. Repeat **their** pronunciation with a querying tone of voice. This may be enough to jog their memory and their second attempt may be nearer the mark or even spot-on. This is because the right information is lodged in the brain; it may be just a matter of strengthening the lines of retrieval. To treat all errors as revealing inability does a great disservice to those trying to learn.

INCORRECT ISN'T NECESSARILY ENTIRELY WRONG

One stage of poor retrieval skills that many pupils go through can be clearly pinpointed by the fact that they retrieve the right letters but they put them in the wrong order.

In one of the English examples given on page 14 a pupil had written down the task instruction as 'Wright a senten to a penfirend'.

- 'Wright' is an unnecessarily complicated grapheme, possibly resulting from a merger between 'write' and 'right'. But at least it successfully reproduces the correct sound.

- 'A senten' is probably misheard. The task was not to write a single sentence. Was it possibly 'Write eight sentences'?

- But 'penfirend' cannot be said to reproduce the intended sound. It is more likely evidence of muddled retrieval.

The word has probably been encountered for the first time in school rather than in life outside. It has been learnt; the letters are there inside the head, but unfortunately, when they are retrieved, they reappear in the wrong order. As no automatic checking of writing appears to be going on, the mind moves onto the next activity and the error goes unnoticed. How many of our pupils are experiencing this when they write '*chein*' or '*souer*', '*zhen*' or '*zwie*', '*cautro*' or '*beunos*' for '*chien*', '*sœur*', '*zehn*', '*zwei*', '*cuatro*' and '*buenos*'?

We can all recognise this state of not looking at what we are writing; we are often thinking way ahead of the actual words we are writing. Some people become confused and they start to add words or parts of words being thought to words being written. Or they jump from the beginning of one sentence to the end of another and as a result they telescope ideas. They think they have written a complete sentence because the words have gone through their brain. But in fact they have actually missed words out. This can also apply to letters within words; both appear in this example: '*Ma maison est assez grade. Ma chambre. Nous avons une cuisine ...*' (Year 8 pupil).

This extract from what was otherwise an extended piece of writing with remarkably few errors, reveals an interruption to the line of thought. Perhaps the pupil was distracted by something, perhaps he daydreamed for a few minutes; whatever the cause, the result is clear. That the misspelling '*grade*' is not through lack of knowledge but through a momentary lapse in attention becomes clear later on when he is capable of writing: '*Nous avons deux assez grands jardins*'.

The '*grade*' is well thought through enough to have the correct feminine agreement. The loss of the '*n*' and then subsequently the entire meaning of the next sentence beginning '*Ma chambre*' can be put down to a severe lapse in concentration and, what is more important, is evidence that **the pupil did not re-read what he had written.** Had he done so, the omissions would surely have been picked up.

THE BENEFITS OF BEING ABLE TO READ ALOUD

It sounds such an obvious statement: He should have re-read what he had written, then the omissions, i.e. errors, would have been picked up. Children are probably encouraged to do this from their earliest schooldays. But why? Why is the re-reading of writing an effective means of spotting errors?

I believe that reading aloud, whether externally or internally, works as a means of checking for mistakes and omissions because the brain's ability to store is better than our conscious ability to retrieve. By matching what we write against what has been stored in our brain, we can immediately spot errors, whether misspellings or omissions or words in the wrong order – all those kind of mistakes that low levels of concentration when writing might cause.

Apocryphal stories abound in staff rooms of whole classes copying down complete nonsense from the board and only realising their mistake when one of them is asked to read the text aloud. The mind is not necessarily engaged when one is copying writing. The mind, as we have seen above, can be easily distracted when writing. But in order to re-read aloud what has been written, one's eyes need to follow the words one by one. If these are sounded out, either aloud or internally, then misspellings, poor structuring and omissions seem to leap from the page. Time and time again I have seen pupils correct their own work, just because they have been encouraged to re-read it aloud. This must indicate that the brain has stored somewhere the correct pattern of sound or cadence of the sentence structure and the correct 'look' of the word and the act of reading aloud gives the brain the chance to match the two.

In the vital initial stages of foreign language learning, by listening to, and therefore inputting into our brains, the sound of target-language words, phrases and sentences, we are building up an aural store of pattern and intonation and cadence and a visual store of spellings on which we can later rely.

So we should be giving pupils plenty of opportunity to listen to the sound of the language and to repeat sounds and structures aloud – either internally or externally. **The next recommendation is therefore – develop the habit in your pupils of checking whatever they write by reading it aloud – either out aloud or in their heads.**

BUILDING THE INNER EAR

Pupils should be encouraged to recall and practise sound in their head before they say a word or phrase or a sentence aloud. This can be easily achieved in class and should become a regular instruction.

Répète le mot à voix basse/à toi.	*Sag das Wort innerlich.*
Tu peux entendre le mot dans ta tête?	*Kannst du das Wort innerlich hören?*
Repite la palabra en voz baja.	*¿Puedes oirla en tu cabeza?*

 ## DISCRIMINATING SOUNDS

Pupils need to practise seeing a word or phrase and selecting the right sound for it. This exercise makes excellent use of a machine like the Language Master, where blank cards, i.e. with no visual prompt at all, can be recorded with single words or phrases. The pupils are given a list of words or phrases to find and have to play the various blank cards through the machine. They set aside those with the sounds that match the words on the list. As pupils become better at 'hearing' words, 'red herrings' should be recorded to distract them.

Language Masters are unfortunately not as common as CD-ROMs have become. Many, if not most, CD-ROMs designed for initial language learning offer endless repetition and manipulation of exercises where any two of three attributes of the vocabulary are given in order to test the third, i.e.:

- See a picture; hear a word; select from a list the correct word.
- See a picture; select the correct word from a list; hear the answer.
- Hear a word; select a picture; see the written word.
- Hear a word; select the written word; see the picture.
- Hear the word; repeat the word; hear the word again.

To make best use of CD-ROMs, your ICT room needs to be fitted with headphones, if pupils are to benefit from regular practice. Use a CD-ROM vocabulary exercise as a starter for ICT lessons; they also allow pupils to work at their own pace, practising listening, reading and speaking. If the vocabulary does not exactly fit the coursebook, it doesn't matter. What is important is that the pupils are developing the new target-language phonic system.

 ## POINTING OUT MISTAKES

There is nothing pupils like better than correcting a teacher. So encourage the following:

- using a well rehearsed list of vocabulary or a text from a course book, begin reading aloud, deliberately mispronouncing some of the words;
- pupils have to shout out '*Erreur!*' or '*Falsch!*' '*¡Un error!*' whenever they hear a word mispronounced.

This is an especially useful exercise if you make use of mispronunciations that you have heard pupils use or you exaggerate any prevailing English accents.

The next best thing to correcting a teacher is correcting a friend. So once they have corrected you, ask one of them to do the reading aloud. If you don't like the idea of encouraging pupils to make deliberate errors, remember – to intentionally make a mistake, you have to be very aware of **what is right.** Try it out with older pupils first. They won't find it easy.

DEALING WITH LOOK-A-LIKES

Many European languages contain a large percentage of words that appear to make learning easy – because they look exactly like or very similar to an English word and very often have the same or similar meaning.

Far from making learning easy, look-a-likes can cause problems throughout language learning careers, but especially at the beginning.

At the very moment when a teacher is trying to develop in the pupils a different phonic system, it is crucial that constant emphasis is given to words that are instantly recognised and understood. If they are taken for granted, then they will be taken as read … **in English**!

For example: many coursebooks start off with a unit on personal details, in which pupils are introduced to first names. For example:

From *Actif I* (LCP)	From *Mach's gut* (Nelson Thornes)	From *Caminos I* (Nelson Thornes)
Charlotte	Karin	Isabel
Philippe	Sebastian	Elena
Thomas	Anna	David
Charles	Christoph	Carlos
Nicholas	Karl	Luis
Paul	Daniel	Erica

Here are more examples of look-a-likes:

From *Actif I*, Unité I (LCP)	From *Mach's gut*, Lektion I (Nelson Thornes)	From *Así I* (Nelson Thornes)
Un crayon	*Der Tiger*	*Geografía*
Un dictionnaire	*Die Giraffe*	*Biología*
Une disquette	*Der Wolf*	*Inglés*
Une table	*Der Leopard*	*Música*
Une gomme	*Der Hund*	*Religión*
Un stylo	*Die Ratte*	*Matemáticas*

In fact it is only in the **written** form that these words are instantly recognisable. In the **spoken** form they are not at all as easy to discern. Turn this to your advantage and use them as listen/recognising/pinpointing exercises.

If we do not emphasise the difference in sound, we cannot be surprised if, for ever and a day, our pupils pronounce them *à l'anglaise* … and at the same time have great difficulty in recognising them when heard. This is particularly true of French, where a glance at vocabulary introduced over the first term will reveal a high percentage of look-a-likes. Using their English **reading** skills, pupils will recognise these words when met for the first time and unless we take pains to tie these existing skills to new sounds, then, when the word is needed, it will be recalled via the English system – no new target-language system having been created for it.

Here, I would suggest, lies the most probable cause of the problem quoted above on page 10 about the influence of the written word on pronunciation. **English pronunciation will rule – if we do not insist on replacing it or adding to it the elements of the target-language system for pronunciation.**

A reply which contains a word spoken in an English accent during the GCSE oral exam is given 0 marks. A rough count of the number of answers that could be expected to contain such words in an ordinary exam can be as high as 25%.

For example:

famille/Familie/familia   camping/Campingplatz   hôtel/Hotel/hotel   sandwich, el fútbol, etc

We could therefore improve our pupils' oral exam mark by as much as one quarter just by insisting throughout the five years that they never ever sound a word that looks like English as an English word.

The recommendation is: Make a deliberate effort from the start to focus on look-a-likes. You must get across to pupils that if it looks like English, it will not sound like English. Exercises should be carried out consistently over the five years of language learning.

THE 'BLACKBOARD OF THE BRAIN'

The importance of developing internal sound and vision during the early stages of language learning cannot be underestimated A research programme that was included in the Channel 4 programme *Mystery of the senses* revealed the following.

The producer, Diane Ackermann, was placed in a scanner, so that the activity of her brain could be monitored and recorded. She was then read a list of simple items such as 'Apple. Bird. Ball. Dog …', etc; she had to imagine the object, i.e. 'see' it in her imagination and say 'yes' as soon as the image was clear in her mind. Then the same list was re-read, but this time she was shown a picture of each item as the name was read out. So now her brain had to match the sight of an object with the sound of its name, rather than just locate the meaning and the image of a sound within her brain.

What was remarkable was that the activity pattern of the brain hardly differed during the two exercises. When conjuring up the image of each word into her imagination, that part of the brain that controls sight was nearly as fully active as when it was consciously matching an externally seen object with the sound of the word. The conclusion drawn was that internal sight is as much 'seeing' as external sight.

This is important for us, because as language teachers we have to build up a new system of word recognition in the target language so that:

- pupils can recognise words externally, i.e. when reading; and
- so they can recall words accurately, when they want to say or write them.

If the same parts of the brain are responsible for both, then by developing the one, we may well be simultaneously developing the other. If we can recall accurately a word to our mind's eye, then we will have no difficulty in recognising that same word when we see it externally. What is more, when we see it externally, we should be able to recognise whether or not it is spelt correctly by checking it against the internal version.

I have always referred to this ability to 'see' in the mind's eye as 'the blackboard of the brain'. I used to ask my pupils to very deliberately write words and phrases to be learnt on this 'blackboard', sometimes even specifying the type and colour of lettering against another colour background. When recalling words or meanings, I would ask them to shut their eyes and retrieve the word letter by letter or draw the picture on this inner space as a deliberate step in the recall process. This can be a useful ploy to pass on to pupils, who are having difficulty learning new words.

REVERSING THE PROCESS

Many of the exercises suggested in Chapter 2 can be extended or adapted so that the listening and matching exercises are immediately followed by reading aloud exercises.

☐ **The list game:** as already suggested, as soon as pupils show themselves adept at picking out words as you sound them, hand over the selection to one of them and get them to call out a new list of words.

☐ **Look-a-likes:** these need years of practice. Hand out a list of new look-a-like vocabulary; ask the pupils to practise by themselves silently; then, ask for volunteers to read the words aloud as they think they should be pronounced. As the correct sound has not yet been heard, they have to dig deep into their experience and the sounds stored in their brains to do this activity.

This same principle can also work as a group or pair activity. The pupils individually record themselves saying the new words as best they can; then, as a group or as a pair, they listen to a master tape with the correct pronunciations. They then replay their own recordings and have to judge who in their opinion came closest to the correct sound.

☐ **The stand-up sit-down to a story game:** instead of standing up and sitting down, pupils can have more than one word or phrase written on cards. These are turned over face down as they are heard. This exercise is then immediately followed by an oral gap fill exercise in which the teacher pauses in the story and the pupil who holds that phrase on a card, fills in the gap orally. The same can be achieved using **tapescripts:** play a tape three or four times, then turn the volume down from time to time and ask the class or individuals to continue reading aloud. Eventually some pupils will be able to achieve this without a text to follow in front of them! But probably not until they reach Years 9 or 10!

☐ **Practising phonics:** using material similar to the *Bouche/bouge/bougie/bout/bouteille* exercise, pupils have to choose the correct written words from a selection while listening to a tape of the words or phrases. This could be just isolated words or phrases or you could create a complete but brief text which they have to recreate with the word cards. They then reverse the process and re-read aloud the words, phrases or text they have assembled. If another pupil is following the original tape with the headphones half on half off, then any words a pupil stumbles over can be quickly supplied by the other.

☐ **Reporting back**: When working in groups, try pinning the text or sentences to be used around the room. In turn one pupil from each group has to go to the text, read the next line and report it back to the group, who write it down on paper. The 'reporter' in whose mind's eye the correct spellings will still be clear, is only allowed to point out mistakes by repeating the target-language word or phrase that has been written incorrectly.

Throughout the early stages of learning, it should be made clear to the pupils:

• that you are not expecting them to achieve perfection immediately;
• that developing an ear and eye for a new language is not something that will be theirs overnight;
• only through dint of practice and more practice will their brains be able to sort out what they need to know.

You may like to reassure them that once the skills have been developed, then learning will speed up, become easier and more accurate. The benefits may take some time coming, but in the end they will be worth it.

4 Storage and recall

It is only when pupils can recognise the sound of new vocabulary, attach the correct meaning to it, locate it within text and then read the written version aloud, that they should be entrusted with the learning of it by heart. Otherwise too many existing automatic procedures of mother-tongue thought may interfere with their learning.

This means that in the initial stages we ought to be spending much longer than we usually do developing and practising the receptive skills of listening and reading before moving on to the productive skills of speaking and writing. If we take time in the early stages to develop receptive skills, as well as training our pupils in good learning techniques, then, later on as their skills develop we can reduce the amount of time spent on such things without sacrificing the quantity and quality of learning.

In the original MFL Programme of Study it stated that pupils should be taught to:

3b acquire strategies for committing familiar language to memory.

Note that they used the word 'familiar'; obviously they were not expecting pupils to be asked to learn by heart vocabulary that they have only just been introduced to! It is a pity the word was removed in the revision in 1999.

The KS3 MFL Strategy requires that pupils should be taught:

7W7 How to find and memorise the spelling, sound, meaning and main attributes of words.
7L1 How to engage with the sound patterns and other characteristics of the language.

These are also main elements of the revised Programme of Study:

- 1a Pupils should be taught the principles and interrelationship of sounds and writing in the target language.
- 3a Pupils should be taught techniques for memorising words, phrases and short extracts.

HOW DO PUPILS LEARN?

I wonder if you have ever asked your pupils how they learn their vocabulary. I began to do this on a regular basis with pupils in both Key Stages, after I had listened to pupils in Key Stage 4 who were utterly disenchanted with foreign language learning and who were threatening to give up on the subject altogether. I asked one of them what the problem was:

Pupil:	There are so many words I don't understand.
Me:	How many new words do you teach yourself every week?
Pupil:	(in amazement) What? What do you mean?
Me:	How many words do you learn a week?
Pupil:	Depends on what we're doing in class – I suppose.
Me:	What do you mean? When do you learn new words?
Pupil:	I just pick them up in class.
Me:	And is that enough? Can you expect to understand just by picking words up in class? How many new words or phrases do you think you should be learning every week?

There then followed a general class discussion about how large a vocabulary would be needed to get through GCSE and how many words would you have to learn per week over the five years to have a good enough vocabulary (the answer is ten to fifteen!). But the pupil was still complaining:

Pupil:	But they're hard to learn!
Me:	Why? How do you learn them?
Pupil:	I look at the paper they're written on.
Me:	And …?
Pupil:	Well … I look at them … I take the paper out … maybe two … three times in an evening and look at them.
Me:	And that's enough? You can learn them like that?
Pupil:	Oh no! I don't learn them like that. That's why it's hard.
Me:	Then why do you go on doing it like that? Why don't you do something else?
Pupil:	[surprised] How else can you learn them?

Her friends immediately started telling her how they learnt their vocabulary. Their methods ranged from writing them out over and over again to getting a friend or family to test them. The pupil complaining was quite surprised. It apparently had not dawned on her in four years of language learning that to continue with a method of learning that wasn't working, was pointless. The idea of changing her method had never crossed her mind. Perhaps she had never had her attention drawn to other possible ways of learning. Perhaps it had just been taken for granted that from the age of eleven onwards she would know how to learn by heart. What was more saddening was the fact that her poor methods of learning had resulted in her being judged as a naturally poor learner and no extra effort appeared to have been made to make her a better one.

We are fortunate today to have plenaries at the end of lessons: see basic lesson plan page 72, Section 3, Appendix 1 *Framework for teaching modern foreign languages: Years 7, 8, and 9* (DfES 2002) where problems such as this can be raised openly and discussed by the whole class. Pupils should be asked frequently during plenaries about any specific difficulties they are encountering and whether they need help. Once a problem has been identified, always throw the next part of the plenary open to the class before coming up with suggestions yourself. Some pupils learn best from their peers.

ARE YOU AN EARS OR AN EYES PERSON?

The means and methods people use to install information in their brains are about as varied as people themselves. Some people – very few – appear to take on board effortlessly all they can see and hear. They can reproduce it faultlessly from the word 'Go' and make use of it immediately. Some put this down to having a photographic memory; others show almost total aural recall. But they are few and far between. Most of us need to make an effort.

There are broadly two different schools of methodology – those that like to listen to words and recall aurally and those that like to see or write the word and recall visually. And there is a large percentage in the middle who use a bit of both. So any common learning method applied in class should encompass both these. **Either the written work should be well supported by sound or the aural work well supported by text.** At times, though, individual exercises may tend more to one than the other, as in the fan-fold method mentioned below. But if the learning by heart is delayed until such times as the sight and sound have been welded together by constant practice and reinforcement, then, whatever the pupil does in order to impress vocabulary into his or her memory, we will have minimised the threat of the written word not being attached to the correct sound or the heard word not being attached to the correct written word.

What follows presumes that vocabulary has been introduced to the class, has been practised, played around with, reinforced and that the skills discussed in the two previous chapters are now in place. Depending on the class ability and the favoured methodology of the teacher, more or less time may have been spent getting pupils to a point where you feel that the learning by heart can now take place.

ON THE LOOK-OUT FOR ERROR

The recommendation here is: do not trust the copying skills of your pupils. When the class is writing new words down for learning by heart, walk around the classroom and check, check, check! How ever often you may have said the words, how ever often they might have seen the words, when pupils come to copy them down, you still have to check – as they are writing – what they are writing.

I once watched a Year 8 pupil dispense with common sense and believe that his eyes were reading '*géagraphie*' from an OHT, rather than suppose that the teacher had made a mistake – actually the writing was small and the OHP pen rather too blobby. When I asked him to check what he had written, he still read the OHT as saying '*géagraphie*'. When I asked him if it was likely that the word 'geography' would suddenly change its spelling like that, he replied: 'It's French, so it might.' A perfectly reasonable answer for someone, who has never been introduced to the influence of Greek roots on European vocabulary or who has not had the similarities/differences between French and English vocabulary highlighted. When I asked him how it was pronounced, he was able to say the word correctly and yet he still maintained that it could be spelt '*géa …*' even when sounding like '*géo …*'

Constantly monitoring pupils' work as they produce it and querying errors as they occur, has often provided me with pupils' most revealing misconceptions – ideas that would never have dawned on me as a teacher and the written evidence of which would normally be put down to poor learning, rather than a misunderstanding.

It is a fact that in the early stages of second and foreign language learning pupils can be creating the weirdest and wildest theories and hypotheses about the new language they are tackling. Many of these are caused by a single concept, one shared by many, if not most, learners of foreign languages.

> *The naive learner beginning his first foreign language lesson starts from the hypothesis that the foreign language basically functions in the same way as his own language with only the lexical items being different.* (Ringbom 1987)

We have all seen the results of this belief – transliteration. It is especially common during pupils' first efforts at free writing.

'Ich bin gehen' for 'I am going'	*'Je suis onze ans'* for 'I am 11'
'Ich bin heisse' for 'I am called'	*'Mein Bruder's Zimmer'* for 'my brother's room'

In extreme cases it can override the evidence of their own eyes and make them read what they think they are seeing, rather than what is actually there.

During the summer term, i.e. after two terms of learning, during which time the following phrases must have been seen, copied, said and written umpteen times, I watched a very bright Year 7 pupil copy down a dialogue from the board like this:

Bonjour! Je'm appelle Marie. Et toi?
Bonjour. Je'm appelle Luc. Tu as des frères ou des sœurs?
Oui. J'ai un frère. Il's appelle Jean. J'ai une sœur. Elle's appelle Anne.

At this point I asked the pupil to check what he had written with what was on the board. He did so and couldn't see anything wrong. As I knew he knew about apostrophes and their uses, I asked him to check these in particular. He did so and still couldn't see anything wrong. I then pointed out the misplaced apostrophes and explained why they were needed where they should be. He replied:

'Oh. I thought it was like the English. 'I'm called' so *'Je'm appelle'*. I'm = *Je'm*
And the same here … *'Il's appelle'* is 'He's called'. He's = *Il's* …'

I wonder how many mistakes made by our pupils have as conscious and clear a reason behind them as that. Uncorrected, he would soon have been retrieving from his memory *'Je'm grand'* in the same way the pupil mentioned in Chapter 1 retrieved *'je m'appelle grand'*.

Small wonder then that those pupils, who don't even understand what use an apostrophe serves in English, can be seen to copy them down at random or even, which I have very commonly observed, mistake them for commas or accents and vice versa.

Il,'sappelle	*J'mapple*	*Je'mappelle*	*J' mappelle*	*Je ' m appelle*
fre're	*pe're*	*pre's*	*'a or a' (for à)*	

CONTROLLING INPUT

In order to avoid elementary copying errors, I recommend using the fan-fold method. I print on one half of a landscape A4 sheet a table with as many rows as words to be learnt and between seven or eight columns across the sheet. The vocabulary is entered by me in the first column on the left-hand side. I then copy this table below so that I can print out two tables per A4 sheet. Hand out a table to each pupil.

die Maus die Katze der Hund der Vogel das Kaninchen das Pferd						

Before the sheet goes home, the English meanings are entered into the second column and these are then checked by the whole class. I also check that the English spellings are correct.

Now the sheet goes home for homework. The technique is known as fan-fold. First of all column no. 1 is folded over so that only the English meanings in column no. 2 are visible. The pupils write down as best they can from memory the target-language words in column 3.

	mouse cat dog bird rabbit horse	die Mause die Kazte die Hunt die Fogle die Kanenhen die Pfert				

Having finished, they open up the hidden column 1, check and correct their answers as necessary. Then columns 1 and 2 are folded over leaving the target-language words in column 3 visible. Now the English meanings are written down in column 4. When finished, these are checked and corrected against the information in column 2. And so on across the sheet, folding over one more column each time and entering in alternately target-language words and their English meanings.

die Maus die Katze der Hund der Vogel das Kaninchen das Pferd	mouse cat dog bird rabbit horse	die Mause die Kazte Katze die Hunt der Hund die Fogle der Vogel die Kanenhen das Kaninchen die Pfert das Pferd	mouse cat dog bird rabbit horse	die Mause die Katze der Hund dieer Vogel dieas Kanin das Pferd	mouse cat dog bird rabbit horse	die Maus die Katze der Hund der Vogel die Kaninchen das Pferd

The sheet is then stuck into the exercise or vocabulary book as a record of learning. The first benefit is that a teacher can be assured that the learning homework has been done. And the pupils can 'show off' that they have indeed done their homework! Secondly, pupils with poor copying and checking techniques can be easily spotted when the teacher checks these learning sheets. These pupils will need extra help and guidance before they can be left to do such work alone successfully.

And thirdly, the greater percentage of pupils will have the meanings and the better part of the correct spellings firmly lodged in their minds after this exercise.

 ## LEARNING ALL THE WORDS

Make sure that in any vocabulary learning, look-a-likes are included. '*La table*' still needs its gender and its pronunciation learnt, even if its meaning is clear.

When giving out vocabulary to be learnt, a long list can be reduced to manageable proportions by sorting the words into four groups: hand pupils a small A5 piece of paper; let them divide it into four and write the headings: *exactly like / almost like / different meaning / nothing like*. Read and write up the words to be learnt and get the pupils to write them in one of the four boxes.

- Those that are instantly recognisable because they are spelled the same and have the same meaning.
  – These must be learnt for sound and gender.

- Those that look nearly like English and have the same meaning.
  – These must be learnt for spelling, sound and gender.

- Those that look exactly like or nearly like English and have different meanings.
  – These must be learnt for meaning as well as sound and gender.

- Those that look nothing like anything you know.
  – These must be learnt for meaning, spelling, sound and gender.

exactly like	almost like
different meaning	nothing like

When testing vocabulary discretely, you can make use of these categories.

- Words from group i) = Call them out in the target language. Can they recognise and spell these words?
- Words from group ii) = Call them out in English. Can they write them in the target language?
- Words from group iii) = Call out in the target language. Can they write down the English meaning?
- Words from group iv) = Test in any of the conventional ways.

Some topics will throw up more look-a-like vocabulary than others. This does not make the topic any easier. It just means that the emphasis on learning is different.

Practising look-a-likes has to be continuous throughout the five-year period. In Key Stage 4 I have found brochures and other forms of realia very useful. I have even used a paper placemat from McDonald's with a Year 10 group. All the food on offer was pictured on it, each clearly labelled. The task was to practise their French accents by ordering a snack. It took them a good deal of effort and concentration to say 'Chicken McNuggets', 'Milkshake' and 'Cheeseburger' in an acceptable French accent!

CALL

Computer Assisted Language Learning (CALL) has unfortunately fallen into disfavour over the last few years, having been ousted by more appealing ICT activities such as accessing the Internet and making use of word processors for writing. Some departments are investing heavily in complete packages that support either a coursebook series or a level of language learning, which offer whole class exercises as well as individual practice on a CD-ROM. But I do not know of any package that has as a basis CALL, i.e. using the computer to actually learn rather than practise the vocabulary word by word.

If given the chance and the software, it is the one activity that I would use before I sent any work home to be learnt. I would try to book at least 30 minutes in the computer room for all Key Stage 3 classes, on a regular basis – once a week or once a fortnight – especially during those vital first few terms of language learning. But the immediate problem is finding the correct software. There are plenty of free activities and exercises on the Web but not all of them have a suitable pedagogic basis: they are more often than not tests rather than learning programs; their content is not necessarily exactly what you want. Even those programs such as *Hot Potatoes* or *Quia* which a teacher can author to suit his or her own classes, only offer reinforcement under the guise of testing exercises: the initial introduction and learning has got to have taken place before they can be tackled.

During the first experimental years of computers in schools in the early 80s I tried out any number of computer programs on the market. I very quickly noticed that a certain vocabulary learning program seemed to be benefiting the pupils – Kosmos' *French Mistress* and *German Master*. My initial observations and conclusions were borne out by subsequent practice. Pupils' behaviour became so predictable that when I became an advisory teacher I knew I could introduce this program to unknown pupils, whose teaching I had not in any way influenced, and yet I could still anticipate their actions and reactions to this program. Why? It has taken me many more years to unpeel the possible reasons that underpin the important and, I believe, unique contribution the computer can make.

This particular program is still available but has not, to my knowledge and regret, been re-written for the latest PCs. It makes it look rather old fashioned – which is a pity as it was very pupil friendly – pupils don't appear to mind making mistakes on it – because, as they tell me, 'You can always have another go and get better at it.' This is encouraging and motivating and also revealing of our own prejudices about software as opposed to those of our pupils: they do not necessarily desire all-singing all-dancing programs, just ones that give them the opportunity to succeed!

Instead of setting pupils to compete against each other, the computer encourages them to compete against themselves. Instead of testing them once only and judging their ability on that test, it allows them to go over and over the same test, removing errors until perfection or near perfection is attained.

Pupils can do three things during this program in order to spell the word or phrase required:

- They can enter the letters confidently – because they know them and are right;
- They can enter them confidently or less so – because they think they know them but are wrong;
- They can decide that they don't know how to start or how to continue to spell a word and ask for a hint by pressing the TAB or COPY key which will fill in the next letter.

At the end of the exercise the number of mistakes and hints are listed. Each time pupils try the exercise, their aim is to decrease the numbers: I have never met a pupil yet who failed to do this over a 30-minute lesson. They may have made 25 errors and needed fifteen hints on their first go, but by the end of the lesson, three or four or more goes later, they are happily recording only four errors and two hints, maybe even a clear round.

No conventional vocabulary test I know of is willingly undertaken by pupils so many times in quick succession, with the express intention of getting fewer errors. But then no conventional vocabulary test informs the pupil immediately that the last letter written is wrong. No conventional test can feed a pupil a word letter by letter until the recall process occurring in the brain is suddenly able to fill in whatever is missing or whatever it can, even if it is only a letter or two and still be given credit for it.

This program's unique feature is that it gives instantaneous correction. This is one of the two important factors that made me remain with this program for over fourteen years. Time and time again I have stood behind a group of pupils and listened to them as they try the exercise for a second or third time.

- 'No! Not that! It's an 'e'. Remember you put 'a' last time and we were wrong. It's an 'e'. or
- 'Don't you remember – we did that last time and nothing happened. It's not right ... What is then?'
- 'I don't know. I'm not sure. But I know it's not that ...'
- 'Try TAB again, cos I don't know either.'

I call this the power of negative learning. By allowing pupils to put down what they believe to be right, by then telling them immediately whether they are right or not and then letting them repeat the test over and over again so as to eliminate their errors, it becomes clear that the force of immediate correction is a powerful mind-check in all subsequent goes.

I have recently found that neuroscience research is proving this to be true. When new information is received by the brain through one, some or all of the senses, multiple random connections are made to existing neurones. Those connections that are revisited through reinforcement or practice within a short period of time are strengthened: those that are not, fade and are lost. By creating a reminder in the short term memory to avoid revisiting a wrong answer, the pupil no longer 'goes down that road' and so the connection is weakened. Once it is no longer used, the actual physical connection disintegrates and the connection to the wrong answer is lost.

The potential of a computer program to be immediately available once again from the beginning also plays to the natural learning techniques of the brain. 'Neurons that fire together, wire together' (Edelman 1987). By repeating the same exercise and avoiding wrong answers, the connections to the right answers are strengthened until they become automatic reactions and retrievals. The more often the pupil repeats the right answer, the more solid the neural pathway that retrieves that answer from the brain. Baroness Greenfield summed up the process succinctly when she said 'Use it or lose it' (Greenfield 1997).

It is not surprising then that frequent use of this program sharpens pupils' accuracy, by preventing continued use of wrong retrieval processes and replaces them with correct procedures, which can be developed to such a pitch, that they become automatic responses.

The traditional vocabulary test is by all accounts a very unsatisfactory method of learning. Our corrections will be made at home that evening and it may take two or more days before the tests are handed back. The mistakes are obvious; they are marked in red. The corrections are not necessarily so obvious: we rarely have time to write in the correct answer. I have yet to see pupils intently looking at their mistakes and then making a mental note of their errors. Because there is no immediate need, no mental 'warning tag' is put against any of the mistakes.

To pupils only 10/10 is a satisfactory result. Even 9/10 or 8/10 is not good enough for them. As for 4/10 or less – well it just goes to show that you're pretty hopeless at this subject, doesn't it?

(When the acknowledging of results is inevitable, I always start from one and work upwards. 'Who got one or more right?' All hands go up 'Two?' 'Three?' 'Four?' and maybe a few hands start creeping down, but at least they have had acknowledged the few that they were able to learn. I encourage those who constantly get low marks by saying that 0/10 is what they should get if they hadn't learnt anything. And then I suggest other ways that might make learning more fruitful.)

By using this computer program, I have children crowing with delight because they have reduced the number of errors from 25 to 12. 'I'm going to have another go and get it down to below ten, Miss!' I have watched the change in children who have sat at the back of the class since primary school, quite happily accepting the judgement of their teachers that they are poor learners but who, when put on a computer by themselves, have, in the end, to think for themselves. They have turned round beaming to report 'Miss, I've only made 30 errors this time … down from 65.' Just imagine that pupil's result on a conventional test. It would have confirmed her worst doubts – that she was no good at this subject. **Here on the computer 30 errors out of a possible 175 letters instead of 65 out of 175 looks exactly what it is – progress!**

INCOMPLETE RETRIEVAL

The other important factor in this program was the use of the TAB key – the hint. Once again I have frequently witnessed children searching their brains for the spelling of a word which they can say quite happily: they can remember some of it but not all of it.

The screen is showing:

my sister

The group confidently enter '*m*'.
One of them is about to enter '*o*' when stopped by another.
'No! Not '*mon*'! It's an '*a*' – '*ma*' '*ma sœur*'.
No. 3 agrees and the '*a*' is dutifully and correctly entered; as is the '*s*' of *sœur*.
'It's '*o*' '*u*' '*e*' '*r*', isn't it? suggests No. 1.
'No, it's '*u*' '*o*' '*e*' '*r*'.' contradicts No. 2.
And No. 3 chips in with 'I'm not sure. Let's TAB it.'

They press the TAB key and the '*o*' appears.
'See', says No. 1 triumphantly, 'I was right. Now it's '*u*' and the key is pressed but nothing happens.
'No, it's not. See that's a mistake. Don't do it again.
'What is it then? '*s*' '*o*' …?'
'Shall we TAB?' says No. 3, who is obviously very unsure.
'I think it's that funny '*e*'. It's part of the '*o*'. Try '*e*'.
No. 1 is not convinced 'Nah! It's not '*e*'! '*s*' '*o*' '*e*' … looks dead silly. Try TAB!'

With two out of three now in agreement, TAB is pressed and produces the disputed '*e*'.

They have to TAB to get the '*u*' as well but are able to finish off with the '*r*'.

So their first effort has result in three TAB keys out of five letters. Or to put it more positively 2/5 letters right! Just because they can say the word, they may not be able to spell it correctly; they know all the letters; it's just they can't quite recall the order of them yet.

I have seen children writing '*frère*' like this. They TABbed the '*f*', added the '*r*', TABbed the '*è*' and happily and confidently added '*re*'. Three letters correct out of five.

I have seen children having to TAB '*c*' '*o*' '*c*' '*h*' before the brain supplies '*-on*'.

I have seen them enter '*Il*', add an '*s*' and make, to their surprise, '*Ils*'; they then enter '*s'appelle*' after some deliberation among themselves, but have to TAB in the '*nt*'.

This has to be a midpoint in retrieval tactics of the brain. We can 'see' the whole word well enough to get an idea of it and even to say it, but the actual letter by letter recall is less secure – just as in the 'penfirend' example given earlier. However, if pupils can be given what they're not sure of or what they know they don't know, then the filling in of what they do know or think they know becomes an encouraging and positive feature.

In a French children's *Playbook* I found the following exercise:

```
p*pe      *renouille      *oleil      lun*      â*e
```

(from *Initiation aux mots; Gommettes et jeux:* 5 (Editions fleuris)

Wouldn't this be a comforting first-step exercise for those who are having to develop memorising tactics? For those who, in my experience, need the use of some kind of external 'TAB key' or prompt for some considerable time because either they lack the confidence needed to risk making a mistake, or because they really have had poor learning experiences up till now. Never having been asked to learn by heart before, they find it difficult to suddenly be asked to store and retrieve accurately.

Having practised adding one letter to complete the word, the French activity book then progressed on to adding in syllables.

(from *Initiation aux mots; gommettes et jeux:* 5 (Editions fleuris)

Not only does an activity like this reinforce in a pupil's mind where the syllable breaks are in a word, but it may also play a part in the development of recall. Just at that stage where the whole word is stored but the retrieval lines are not yet well established, we can use exercises like this to jog the recall system into retrieving the missing part of the word.

If pupils can do such exercises, then you can be assured that the storage at least is complete. They have to be retrieving the letter or syllable from somewhere! If they can fill in a letter, good. If they can fill in a whole syllable, better. And when at last they can give the whole word, great!

The computer program I used, allowed just this: pupils can fill in the whole word or phrase letter by letter correctly, monitoring each entry as it is made, but they can also TAB in any letter they don't know or are unsure of. **Surely it is better to practise in stages rather than** expecting accurate off-by-heart recall from everyone after a single learning homework, over which we have no control.

AT ONE'S OWN PACE

And what of the more able child? The child who does make the effort to learn accurately or who learns vocabulary easily? What happens to them on the computer, if, after the first go, they achieve no errors and no TABs?

Speed takes over. Once accuracy is achieved, repeating the same exercise over and over again to keep chipping away at one's own previous time can absorb a pupil to such a degree that when the bell rings for the end of lesson, it is greeted with groans of dismay and cries of 'Can't I just finish this one?' I am content because I know the end result will be of more use to them than any feeling they might have had gaining a single 10/10 on a conventional test. I know that when that word or phrase is needed, whether in oral or written work, the recall procedures in the brain, so well honed by constant fast practice, will instantly and accurately spring the correct target-language word or phrase to mind.

Having watched children over fourteen years being able to retrieve single letters of words, more than one letter, beginning bits or end bits of words before finally the whole word, I am convinced that storage in and retrieval from the brain are two separate things, each of which has to be considered separately.

If the storage or input is accurate, then there is a possibility that eventually recall or output will be accurate. But if the storage or input is incorrect or vague or misunderstood or based on a misconception, then there is no possibility at all of the recall ever being accurate.

Once we get the right activities that correctly store vocabulary, then the next step is not necessarily immediate total recall. Instead, we should be anticipating that for many of our pupils accurate recall may be an activity that has to be developed. We have to believe that it can be coaxed from even the most reluctant learner by asking for single letter in-fill, multi-letter in-fill, syllable in-fill and finally whole word recall. We can do this with exercises made for use in the classroom or by searching for computer programs or exercises that allow us to do this.

CHECKING FOR ACCURATE STORAGE

How can we tell whether or not pupils have a word or phrase stored in their heads?

Can they recognise the word when they see it? Can they pick it out from a jumble of others? If they can, then – **yes** – it must be stored in their heads. Use linear word searches or spelling tables.

Linear word search 1

piedtrottinetteavionvoiturechevalautobusbateaucartrainfuséevélohélicoptère

If pupils can see the ends and beginnings of words and can separate them successfully, then they are recognising the whole against some internal mental image of the word. If you don't believe this, try the exercise on the previous page on someone who knows no French at all and see where and why they come unstuck!

Linear word search 2

> trotinetchepiedvioturetrottinetteavionfuseévoiturevelochevaldeautobusabta
> chevabateausecartthélicoptèrehraretrainvèlopeidfuséevoitvéloavointraimer

Move on to linear word search 2 where pupils are deliberately misled by 'almost words' and misspellings. They now have to circle only those words that are spelt correctly.

Exercises like these are much more useful than those more usual square wordsearches. These have the advantage of mimicking the lineality of reading, whereas conventional wordsearch squares sometimes hide words diagonally or even backwards!

A third exercise could give actual breaks between supposed words and pupils have to underline those they now recognise.

> trotinet che pied à vioture trottinette est avion fuseé la voiture velo cheval de autobus abta les va bateau se cart hélicoptère le hrare train vèlo peid fusée voici vélo mon avoin traimer a

Don't be surprised if, for instance, 'a', 'à' and 'des' are ignored. It takes some time before beginners give reading value to anything other than 'information words' as opposed to 'function words'.

Encouraging pupils to look for what they can recognise and understand in among a welter of unknown words is a major first step on the way to reading.

 ## SPELLING TABLES

I first made these up for the class where the boy was sure that the word was '*geagraphie*' and where his friends were copying down words to learn with just as many errors. I noted some of their errors and next day gave them back as a table of possible spellings. All they had to do was underline the correct spelling.

anglias	desin	listoire	allamend	phsysique
anglais	dessign	historie	allemand	physices
englais	dissign	histoire	allemend	physique
onglay	dessin	histiore	allimand	fissique

The results were interesting: a small number each time selected the clearly 'aurally' stored *'listoire'* *'onglay'* *'fissique'*. There was even a small but intensely felt discussion about whether spelling even mattered so long as a word was understood.

I have since found this a very useful exercise. I take errors made by the pupils themselves in a homework, draw up a table, and hand it out **before** the books are returned. Pupils then complete the exercise, have their books returned and then check what they actually wrote in their homework.

Sometimes they are horrified at the silly slips that they have made. The spelling table exercise has clearly shown that they are capable of recognising that *'cheveux'* is the correct spelling. Why oh why then did they write *'chevuex'* in the homework. A doubly useful exercise because it makes pupils look at the corrections to work done in a very focused fashion!

It is just as useful with phrases as with words.

je m'apple	jay abite	j'ai onze ans
je' m' appelle	j'ai habit	jay onse an
je m'appelle	shabeat	je onze an
j' m' appelle	j'habite	jay onze ans

All these are genuine examples of pupil production at the end of Year 7!

As the spellings are all theirs anyway, there is a great deal of 'mind jogging' going on. If you hear a fellow pupil scoffing at the mistake you made, the drive to make sure you don't do it again is greater than any red mark made by a teacher.

CHECKING FOR ACCURACY

I would always choose whole class recall first of all, then team recall, then group or pair and finally individual. I do this by making a set of alphabet cards plus accent cards:

- A number of pupil volunteers are selected to come to the front of the class where the ABC cards are.
- I call out in the target language a word we have been learning and they have to pick out the cards to spell it. The class acts as the checker and points out any mistake by calling *'erreur'* or *'falsch'* or *'¡un error!'*.
- After a few words I hand over to the class and let them call out newly learnt words. Then a new set of pupils goes up to the front and so on.
- The next lesson I divide the class into two or four teams depending on the size of class; each team will have a set of ABC cards and they now compete against each other to see who can arrange the words correctly fastest.
- In the subsequent lesson pupils work in their usual groups of four to six pupils, only this time they have a single sheet of paper between them and they have to write the words down as I call them out in the target language. They are still working as a group because this may

well still be a stage of partial recall for many of them. John can give the beginning bit, Mary chips in with the next letter, Matthew remembers the accent and Simon recalls the end.

- The following lesson I repeat the activity but this time with a sheet of paper between two pupils. Here at least two heads can be better than one.
- And it is only after this session, when we are likely to be almost at the end of the unit, that the 'game' develops into individual response, where each pupil has a sheet of paper and must write the words down as I say them.

Previously known as a spelling test, it will now appear instead as a game. Its gradual build-up has ensured that the slower pupils have benefited from the expertise of their quicker fellow pupils; there has been time to hone the paths of recall in the brain, perhaps not to perfection immediately but with improved learning skills and greater accuracy for sure.

ABC card sets: A statistical analysis of the recurrence of vowels and consonants in various languages would give very different results. German needs many more 'u's than French for example, whereas French and Spanish will need extra 'e's. On a target-language Scrabble board, you will find the proportion of vowels and consonants needed for that language. If at a loss, contact a friend in the country and ask them to check for you! Always have a few extra blank cards with the ABC so that letters can be added if necessary.

All this is good practice and can form regular lesson starters, following the listening exercises, etc. But the best test of recall is just to use the language in class and, if they have learnt it, they will understand. If they really know it and can recall and produce, then they will use it.

Go to the coursebook and see how much they understand. Do some more practice and take them back to the same passage in the coursebook. How much more can they understand?

Let them watch a video for a second or third time. Does it make more sense now?

By just looking at a piece of text on one occasion gives pupils no indication of improvement. It is a mere matter of how much do they or don't they understand. By going back to the same piece after further learning and practice, pupils are given a clear yardstick by which to measure their own progress. The space in between may be as little as a week or as much as a term or even a year; but by re-presenting material to pupils who will, without a shadow of doubt, be able to understand more of it than before, you will be implicitly indicating that language learning is not an instant 10/10 or 0/10 subject, but one that grows and grows and builds on everything that has gone before.

The more they see the same words, whether in the same or different contexts, the more their brains will be asked to recognise and recall them. The more often they are asked to do this, the stronger the paths of cognitive procedure required for that recall will be.

Part 2

Active grammar

5   Language awareness

One of the most misunderstood words in the English language has to be the word 'grammar'. Chapter 6 will discuss the many meanings that this word has accumulated over the years; all that is needed here is to make clear the sense in which it is meant in this particular context.

For my money, no one has defined the word as well as Fredrich Bodmer in his *Loom of language* when he said:

> *Having lists of words you know the usual meaning of, will not get you very far (in a language) unless you have knowledge of another kind.*   (Bodmer 1944; 1987)

It is a very apt definition because it illuminates immediately the gap between the expectations of the average initial learner and reality. If asked what they expect to have to do in order to learn a second language, most will reply: 'Learn words'. It is rare that anyone mentions '… and how to string them together to make sense.'

And yet that is precisely what should be occupying their thoughts at least 50% of the time. Of course they do need to learn words – between ten and fifteen a week as already mentioned. But without that other knowledge, of what to do with the words and how to order them, then all they will be left with is a list of words and a handful of phrases learnt by heart.

The fashion in the 70s and 80s for teaching 'without grammar' did not mean what it said. Grammar cannot be avoided unless you **are** just teaching lists of words. What was meant was 'without explicit grammar'. As the teaching of English grammar waned and the terminology to describe parts of language became as foreign as anything taught as a second language, so pupils understood less and less what they found in the coursebooks. As the teaching of foreign languages themselves spread and overflowed from the academic borders that had held them in a strictly explicit grammatical straitjacket for years, teachers realised that they had a stark choice. Either they taught the grammar from scratch and explained language as language before they moved into the foreign language, or they could adopt different methods in which the grammar patterns could be absorbed implicitly through repetition and use – just as children do with their own mother tongue.

And here we are back at the 'natural learning' theory. Certainly repetition and practice can and do give learners a feel for grammatical structure and usage – under ideal conditions, which are i) the bilingual environment or ii) immersion courses or iii) intensive courses. These are proven facts. But unfortunately our pupils have (mostly) already missed out on the bilingual experience and we do not teach in ideal conditions: contact with our pupils can be as little as 50 minutes twice a week – in which time we can deliver neither an immersion or an intensive course. Rather than spend time investigating the pros and cons of explicit and implicit grammar teaching, let us instead turn the concept round and ask: do we have any evidence that pupils need to know more about:

• language terminology;
• the nature of their own language;
• the nature of the target language?

Do we have any evidence that a lack of knowledge of these three things can or does hinder a pupil's progress? Can we predict that without our intervention, they will fall into certain traps? As in the previous chapters we shall be looking at the evidence as revealed by the pupils themselves both in their work and their comments.

> *Errors aren't just irrational acts. There's a flawed reasoning behind them, but a logic nevertheless which experience will improve.* (Wilson 1999)

BUT I LOOKED IT UP IN A DICTIONARY!

Je bidon faire ça!

Soy ventiladora de los libros de Harry Potter

Bushaltestelle das! sagt Mutti

Every single language teacher must have a store of these wonderful gaffes. They are the bright sparks that illuminate the boredom of marking … if one can understand what they are supposed to mean and that sometimes takes some working out!

Dictionaries are such useful things – unless you don't know the first thing about language and then they are suddenly transformed into linguistic traps. They are more likely to be the source of errors than correct information.

The pupil who wrote the French example looked up the English word in a dictionary and there he saw:

can: (n) bidon (m) pot (m): vb pouvoir (irreg)

He/She knew enough to ignore all the information in brackets, because 'there's no point in looking at it. I don't know what it means.' He then wrote down the French word as given – *bidon. Je bidon faire ça* = I can do that.

If the student of Spanish had been more aware of English and its multiple meanings, he/she might have read on past '*ventilador*' to '*abanico*' – another possibility – to '*aficionado*' or even '*adicto*'. But no! he chose the first word!

The student of German fell into the same trap. He/She looked up the word she didn't know and found:

stop: (n) Bushaltestelle (f): (vb) auf/hören (vb reg. sep.)

It was now a straightforward matter of writing '*Bushaltestelle das! sagt Mutti*'. What could be wrong?

Well, what is wrong is a lack of understanding of what (n) and (vb) mean when met in a dictionary, of what the difference is between their usage and of the difficulties posed by the unique characteristics of the English language.

This lack of basic knowledge is not necessarily the characteristic of the initial learner. In the following example from a Year 11 pupil, knowledge and ignorance go hand in hand.

Le bateau évia

The idea being translated was 'The boat sank'. This pupil was wise enough to know that 'sank' is the past tense of 'sink', so that was the word that was looked up in the dictionary. Unfortunately the (nm.) which appeared next to the word '*évier*' didn't register, but the '*-er*' ending did, so the conclusion was drawn that this was a regular *-er* verb and it was treated accordingly. And so a perfectly accurate Past Historic form was made … of a noun!

UNDERSTANDING ENGLISH FIRST

English unlike other European languages cannot claim to be either a Germanic or Romance language. It is both simultaneously and yet, at the same time, it is neither. Both German and French, the two most widely taught foreign languages in our schools, rely on inflection, gender and agreement, German adhering more strictly to its Indo-European inheritance than French which has managed to rid itself of cases, while keeping strictly to gender and number agreement.

A mish-mash of languages created the English language – Norman French, Anglo-Saxon, Viking, Danish, Celtic – and in doing so some of the patterns from one or other language were retained: for example, we use the German system for verbs, for example, *singen, sang, gesungen* but the French system for emphatic pronouns: 'It's me' not 'I am it'.

Occasionally we retained both. English uniquely has retained two forms of the comparative and superlative: the German 'big, bigger, the biggest' and the French 'beautiful, more beautiful and the most beautiful'.

But in many instances the conflicting patterns were thrown out and we were left with invariable forms. In the process many of those useful indicators that differentiated between the same idea being used for different functions, such as verb or a noun, an adjective or an adverb, were lost. We have retained some that make clear whether we are dealing with an adjective, for example 'large' 'hungry', rather than the adverb 'largely' 'hungrily'; but we have lost many others or they have become confused. Is 'lovely' an adverb or an adjective? What is the connection between 'good' and 'well'? Between verbs and nouns there can be a difference: 'to write' but 'the writing'; one can't say *the write or *to writing but it is difficult to find these examples. It is far easier to find the opposite: examples of where there is no difference in spelling or form between the verb and the noun, one just uses 'the' in front of the one and 'to' in front of the other – the watch/to watch: the air/to air, the table/to table, the earth/to earth, etc.

As a result English more than any other European language contains a plethora of homographs – wind (that blows) and wind (a watch); row (a boat) but row (with your parents); bar (to drink in) and bar (when you are no longer allowed in); fly (the insect) and fly (the plane) and homophones – sew, sow, so; rode, rowed, road; horse, hoarse. The latter caused one student, whose ability in English spelling must have been shaky, to confidently reply to a picture question 'Worauf reitet sie?' 'Sie reitet auf einer Heiser' (She is riding on a hoarse)!

If English pupils are not schooled in the characteristics of their own language before they come into their first foreign language lesson, how are they to be expected to deal with such inconsistencies in their own language. If they are not anticipating that similar spellings can have different meanings or functions, or that similar sounds can be spelt either the same or differently and have totally different meanings and functions, what sense can they be making of the English language? Consider this series of words:

- Bough of a tree, bow of a ship, (homophone but not homograph);
- Bow of a ship, bow before the Queen (homophone but different function);
- Bow before the Queen, bow and arrows (homograph but not homophone);
- Bow and arrows, bow in your hair (homophone, both nouns);
- Bow in your hair, violin bow (homophone, both nouns);
- Violin bow, and a dog that says Bow Wow (homograph but not a homophone).

In a foreign language these would either be totally different words or they would be etymologically related but with different forms.

English	French	German	Spanish
Bow (in your hair)	nœud	Schleife	lazo
Bow (tie)	nœud papillon	Fliege	pajarita
Bow (and arrows)	arc	Bogen	arco
(violin) bow	archet	Bogen	arco
(rain)bow	arc en ciel	Regenbogen	arco iris
Bow (of a ship)	proue	Bug	proa
Bow (before the Queen)	révérence	Beugung	reverencia
Bow Wow	ouâ-ouâ	wau-wau	guau guau

In English they are reduced to two sounds and one spelling for multiple meanings, the seven examples here being nouns, but they could have been verbs. How can pupils, who have not been made explicitly aware of this characteristic of the English language, know which word to pick from those offered by a bilingual dictionary? Furthermore if they have not been introduced to the metalanguage of grammatical function: noun, verb, adjective, adverb, etc: how can they be expected to understand which of the many words on offer to select?

It is not as if it would be boring and dull to be given such an insight into English. After all, British comedy relies for much of its humour on such word play. What fun could be had by primary school pupils if asked to make up sentences such as these … and then illustrate them.

The farmer sewed the fields.   **The wind (*wynd) blue a cross the see.**

To children such sentences appear as fun and nonsense. But an essential lesson **is** being learnt about the nature of the English language: namely, how important it is to thoroughly know any word – its meaning or meanings, its sound or sounds, its spelling or spellings … and its function or functions. **Without this kind of knowledge, no useful purpose can be served by referring to a dictionary, an activity which is now an integral part of the KS3 MFL strategy:**

Pupils should be taught:

7T4   How to use a dictionary and other resources appropriately when working on text.
7W8   How to find out or work out and give the meanings of unfamiliar words.

Pupils cannot be expected to learn how to use a dictionary or the grammar section in a coursebook by trial and error. They need some kind of explicit introduction.

- In order to be able to select the correct target-language word, pupils need to understand firstly the concept behind the meaning of the word and to be able to match it to the subheadings given.

- Secondly in order to select the right meaning of the word, once they have located the correct subheading, they need to know the function of the English word they are looking for and how to find it among the various abbreviations: is it an 's' or 'n' or a 'vb' or 'vr' or 'vt' or 'vi', etc?

All these and many other questions implied by the use of dictionaries, glossaries and grammars, must be answered, if our pupils are not to be left to wander in a world for which they have been given no bearings. In the world of grammar, the signposts are clearly marked; and those of us, who have already covered the ground, know that the paths they point to are short cuts that save time during language learning. But if our pupils cannot read the signs: if they do not see them or, the worst scenario, if the signs do not even register with them as signs, then they may well spend hours ineffectually going round in circles, making no headway at all.

Planning a coherent departmental approach

Our first step must be to ensure departmental continuity across the classes and across the Years; departmental members must agree terms, both in English and in the various target languages taught. Also to be decided is how explicit the department wishes to be.

- Do you wish to set aside a certain amount of time at the beginning of each unit of work in order to introduce the new structures, terminology and patterns to the class?
- Would you prefer to set aside a certain amount of time each week?
- Would you prefer to tackle concepts as they arise in lessons?
- Would you prefer to introduce them implicitly before discussing them explicitly in the plenary at the end of a lesson?
- Do you wish to draw clear comparisons between the target language and English or any other of the languages spoken by your pupils?
- How much, if any, of this can be achieved in the target language?

You may decide to keep to introductions in English and further explanations and active practice in the target language. Some teachers find it simple and straightforward to use target language in the initial stages when the language is limited but then revert to discussions in English as concepts become more complicated. Others prefer to use English throughout. **Whatever your preferred method, plenaries are ideal for this.**

You may wish to implement different practices for different abilities of pupil:

- With high level ability pupils you may be able to use the translator-approach, i.e. you explain and demonstrate in the target language and a pupil or pupils explain in English what you are saying.
- For low ability pupils you may wish to avoid any explicit discussion or naming of parts and rely instead on patterns, colours, jigsaws to support ear and eye in developing an unconscious 'feel' for the language.
- Or you may decide to incorporate into your teaching a clearly defined language awareness element to be delivered in English, which allows pupils to explore language comparatively. This can be especially successful when more than one mother tongue is present in the classroom; it encourages children to offer examples in their mother tongues, which makes for even greater awareness than merely one-to-one correlation with English and a target language.

These decisions cannot be made here; they must be individual to each department; what is common to all, however, is the need for your decisions to be clearly written up in your Scheme of Work as agreed methodology across the Years and abilities. Ideally what you write should be merely a reflection of the way you all approach language teaching. If you unfortunately have members of department, who appear to stand in opposite camps on certain issues, then it is vital that they are encouraged to find a suitable compromise. For the sake of the pupils, there should be uniformity of not only terminology, but when it is to be introduced, how it is to be introduced and how it is to be practised.

- Without reference to the departmental Scheme of Work, draw up two lists of grammatical terms that would constitute a minimum/maximum for pupils in each Key Stage.

- Divide each Key Stage list into lists for each Year.
- Now compare your list with the actual terms used in:
  a   dictionaries which are available to your pupils and
  b   the grammar sections of texts books being used.
- Are your lists comprehensive?
- Have you under- or overestimated what might be required?
- Does your list compare well with the list in the existing Scheme of Work? Does the latter need to be revised?

And when all this is in place, you still need to consider how much of what is taught needs to remain receptive knowledge, i.e. enabling the pupils to make sense of what is heard or read and what must become active knowledge, i.e. applied in speech and writing.

- Are all teachers in the department clear about what aspects of grammar need to be both receptive and active and which just receptive? For example: both receptive and active = gender agreement; just receptive = preceding direct object agreements – for the greater majority of pupils.
- Can you clearly differentiate between those pupils who need a minimum of active grammar and those that need a working understanding? Do you need to differentiate for your pupils at all?
- Are all teachers aware of the time gap between receptive knowledge being taken on board and productive ability being guaranteed? We may cover more than two tenses in the first year of learning but we certainly wouldn't expect simultaneous independent production of those tenses.

It is important to remember that just because we have taught an aspect of grammar, it doesn't follow that pupils can immediately make use of it. They can apply it in carefully constructed exercises but left on their own to produce free writing, the system appears to break down and they slide back into transliteration and mother tongue influence, and seemingly for many many terms after they have been introduced to the correct structures. The suppressing of the automatic mother-tongue language production methods of the brain is apparently a very hard and long fought battle! It is perhaps one we should share with our pupils.

In the early 90s with the Languages for All campaign we advertised MFL learning as fun for all – and never really got round to mentioning the personal effort needed. Did we unintentionally oversell our subject? Did we make it seem too easy a subject? When talking to disenchanted Year 9 pupils, who are on the verge of dropping the subject, I have often found that they have been judging themselves by unrealistic self-imposed yardsticks. After three years of learning a foreign language, they had expected to be able to speak it. The fact that they can't, is to them an indication of how badly they are doing: an indication that they cannot be 'good at this subject' and in the competitive world of 'gaining good GCSEs' their only way forward is to drop this 'difficult' subject.

If you express your surprise at their attitude and take the time to assure them that in fact they are doing very well and are making more than satisfactory progress, they are in turn surprised.

'What! You mean I shouldn't be speaking fluently by now?'
'Do you mean it? I'm OK?'
'I thought I was rubbish. I still can't say what I want to say'.

Such remarks are very revealing. I am convinced such opinions develop because we do not properly explain to our pupils in a direct and straightforward manner the disparity between receptive competence – which can be gained quickly and thoroughly by most pupils – and productive competence, which for a large percentage of our pupils may only ever be attainable in a very limited form. We leave them to make up their own yardsticks which are often as spurious as the hypotheses about gender allocation mentioned earlier.

The origin of the word 'infant' is Latin '*infans*' meaning 'unable to speak'. I would suggest that behind this concept is another very powerful influence on our pupils; one that causes many of them to adopt half hearted attitudes towards foreign language learning, even perhaps one of the major causes for dropping the subject. Just at that critical moment in their teenagehood, when puberty kicks in, when they want to feel as good as possible about themselves, what do we do? We render them speechless! We reduce them to feeling like an infant once again – unable to speak and express themselves. It must be so frustrating – even more so nowadays as the spoken element in classes has a higher profile than ever before! No wonder they (and particularly boys) declare a lack of interest and commitment to foreign language learning.

How can we avoid this? We can't! But we can forewarn our pupils that they are likely to feel this way; that it is natural even for adult learners to feel humiliated by their inability to express their thoughts. If we point out steps for learning, they can monitor their own progress for themselves. And what steps can we use? Well the National Curriculum Attainment Targets make a good start! Render them into pupils-speak and pin them up somewhere prominent, even hand them out as a pupil's guide to learning. At least pupils will know that fluency isn't expected of them in Year 9!

By contrast those teachers who have encouraged pupil self expression from the start and have concentrated on giving pupils the language they **want** to use, have reaped the benefits in increased motivation and interest. As and when pupils start to use the target language, they do not correct every single utterance but rather, like any parent, patiently repeat the phrase correctly. They do not expect immediate application of all that is taught but encourage pupils to find situations in which to use what they have just learnt. They also, like their Canadian colleagues, encourage those pupils to speak who want to and do not force those whose courage is still lacking. So long as the shy are listening and taking in, the teachers have the confidence to know that their time will come – eventually.

Unfortunately the time difference between pupils' individual productive competencies is inimicable to all types of assessment and progression charts. Language learning rarely produces a linear progression: rather it goes in fits and starts, sometimes curling back on itself over and over again, then staying still for a time before leaping ahead in one single bound. Trying to fit this into neat charts and graphs of a whole class's progress goes against the grain but is something that teachers are compelled to do. How nice it would be if we could say about our pupils' progress: ask us in five years!

PLANNING A COHERENT WHOLE SCHOOL APPROACH

So much of what we need to do is mirrored in the demands of the National Literacy Strategy and the KS3 Strategy that it is only logical that we should be working together with the English department, on a homogeneous package aimed at complementing each other's teaching.

The next step therefore, should be to share the burden. Once our MFL department has unified its ideas and has firm guidelines written into the Scheme of Work, we need to talk this through with our English colleagues and make sure we know what pupils will have already covered in the National Literacy Strategy and what is still to be tackled in the KS3 Strategy. For our own purposes we need to know the following:

- Have pupils been introduced to dictionary skills? If so, when?
- What terms are they familiar with? What metalanguage is used with the children?
- Will the children have covered this kind of work in primary school? Can Year 7 pupils be expected to understand the difference between round (prep) round (n) round (adj) and round (vb reg)?
- Will they be continuing this kind of work in English over KS3? If so, how?

And it doesn't end there. It is not just a matter of discovering what terms are used in English, but also whether these agree with the same term used in MFL teaching; sometimes it may be that a totally different word is now more current than one we are used to, e.g. connective as opposed to conjunction or it may be that their word has a very different interpretation.

For example:
The following definitions are taken from both the original and the revised Glossary of Terms on the DfES Standards Site **www.standards.dfee.gov.uk/literacy**.

accent – *Features of pronunciation which vary according to the speaker's regional or social origin … The term accent refers to pronunciation only.*

No mention of diacritic marks! It would be useful if our English colleagues could point out the accents used in English loan words, such as café, pâté, employée.

adjective – *Adjectives have different degrees of intensity*
      nominative   *names the quality (tall)*
      comparative   *describes degrees of quality, etc*

This is from the original glossary and has since been revised! However the description 'nominative' may well have been taught to some primary pupils; if it does appear in their speaking about language, be aware that it might not have the meaning MFL teachers usually give it. It is a mistake for 'nominal'.

tense – *A tense is a verb form that most often indicates time. English verbs have **two basic tenses**, present and past, and each of these can be simple or continuous. **English has no specific future tense**. Future time can be expressed in a number of ways using 'will' or present tenses.*

Linguists apparently understand the word 'tense' to mean a verb form that is a single word such as 'walks' or 'walked' or 'sing' and 'sung'. All the rest – such as 'am walking', 'would have walked', 'will walk' are not 'tenses' as such but' tense forms'.

If pupils are not to be confused by two departments using the same term for different grammatical descriptions or two different words for the same thing, it is essential that a combined mapping exercise is undertaken. It is only once all these questions have been resolved, that one can begin to look at methodology. If these things are not already in place, recommend that the two departments work together to create a complementary scheme of work to ensure that, by the end of KS3, pupils do understand common terminology, can refer with understanding to dictionaries and can make reasoned selections.

PROBING PUPIL'S GRAMMATICAL AWARENESS

In order to reassure ourselves that lessons have been learnt, it is useful during the first few terms to investigate just how much our new pupils really do understand.

Nouns v verbs

To show me they understand the difference between a noun and a verb, I ask Year 7 pupils to cast an eye round the classroom and work out which nouns in the room can very easily become verbs and which nouns cannot. For example: 'the table – to table' (a motion at a meeting); 'the chair – to chair' (a meeting); 'the book – to book' (a room); 'the pen – to pen' (someone a note) but 'the window' cannot be re-used as a verb. One can't window. To some children this kind of language 'game' comes as a revelation. By themselves they would have never have noticed that they were able to do this in their own language. The surprise and dawning comprehension is continued when we take a look in foreign language dictionaries to see how to tell the difference between 'the table/to table', 'the floor/to floor' 'the bag/to bag'. In German the repetitive *-en* verb ending soon becomes clear. In French you can soon start building up columns or groups of verbs with the same endings. For most pupils it will come as a complete surprise that two similar looking words in English have to be translated by such different expressions.

the chair	*Stuhl*	*chaise*	*silla*
to chair	*den Vorsitz füh**ren***	*prési**der***	*presi**dir***
the table	*Tisch*	*table*	*mesa*
to table	*einen Antrag einbring**en***	*dépos**er** un projet*	*present**ar** una moción*
the book	*Buch*	*livre*	*libro*
to book	*buch**en***	*réserv**er***	*contrat**ar***

Talking about tenses

Despite the current definition of the word 'tense' in the NLS glossary, most modern language teachers like to talk about three main tenses, past, present and future. It is worthwhile emphasising the fact that the verb system that pupils are about to learn is in fact easier and more straightforward than the one they use every day in speaking English. But before they are introduced to the new system or when tenses are about to be dealt with explicitly for the first time, it is useful to find out just how much they do know about English – implicitly and explicitly.

This exercise is easiest as an electronic worksheet for pairs of pupils in the ICT room, because the verbs can then be highlighted and dragged into place. It can also be done on the board or OHP by a relay of individual pupils but is not so effective.

Create a file with a table three columns by nine rows, with the headings Past, Present and Future with twelve verb forms from one regular and one irregular English verb respectively.

Past	Present	Future
I have been waiting	Wait!	I will sing
I sing	I sang	I do wait
I have waited	I would have waited	I had sung
I was singing	I have sung	I did wait
I am going to sing	I waited	I will wait
I was waiting	I had waited	I have been singing
Sing!	I would have sung	I did sing
I wait	I do sing	I am going to wait

Ask the pupils to start looking for tense form pairs such as *I have been waiting* and *I have been singing* and to drag them to either the past, present or future column. The discussions that arise are well worth listening to, if you wish to get a measure of how well your pupils understand their own verb system. Here is a partially completed exercise.

Past	Present	Future
I sang I waited	I sing I wait	I will sing I will wait
I was singing	I do sing I do wait	I am going to sing
I was waiting		I am going to wait
I have sung I have waited	I would have waited	I had sung
		I did wait
	I had waited	I have been singing
	I would have sung	I did sing
I have been waiting		

What is the real meaning and purpose of 'I do wait/sing'?

Where do 'Wait!' and 'Sing!' fit?

Is 'I waited' the same thing as 'I sung'?

Can your pupils come up with other tense forms? 'I am singing/waiting' has been deliberately missed out as an easy answer to that question. But can they spot that 'I will have sung/waited' and 'I would sing/wait' are also not there?

Can they name any of the tenses? If not, or if they are unsure or get stuck after a few, suggest some tense names and ask which form might fit that description. Are the names helpful? Present Continuous. Present Perfect? Imperfect? Conditional?

Get them to check in the coursebook's grammar section or the list of irregular verbs in a bilingual dictionary. What tense names are used there? Are they the same?

What is easier – to learn the tense name or to remember the English equivalent? If they choose the latter, ask them what the difference is between 'I would visit Gran this weekend but I've got too much homework' and 'Last year I would visit Gran every weekend'. English isn't at all clear-cut when it comes to verb forms!

Dictionary work

Meet them head-on and pre-empt mistakes by constantly raising pupils' awareness of *double entendre* or differences in function or homographs. If the word '(football) match' is going to be used in the next topic, then have the pupils locate the word 'match' in the class dictionaries. The entries from large modern dictionaries are too long to be reprinted here; here are extracts from two smaller dictionaries: one from Cassell and the other from Langenscheidt respectively.

match *n allumette* (for lighting); *(artill.) mèche f; pareil, pendant, égal* (an equal); *mariage* (marriage); *parti* (person to be married) *m; lutte* (contest) *f; match m, parti m; course* (in running, sailing, rowing etc); *v.t. assortir, appareiller, égaler, apparier* (pairs of things); *rivaliser avec; tenir tête à, se mésurer avec* (to oppose); *v.i. s'assortir, être pareil; convenir, s'accorder, s'harmoniser.*

match ^I   *allumette f.*

match ²   *I Égal m, pareil(le f) m;* colours: *assortiment m;*
    mariage m; sp. match (pl. matchs, matches) *m.*

    2 v/t égaler (q.); rivaliser avec (q.); assortir
    (colours); *unir (q.) (à,* with); *v/i s'harmoniser*

Ask them how many different functions it has: can it be a noun and a verb and a preposition and an adverb, etc? Ask them how many English meanings can they come up with. You could end up with a blackboard looking like this:

	match	
(n)	vb	adj
football match	to match yourself against someone	
match (box)	to match/suit	matching
a (good) match of colours	to match/equal	
a happy match/marriage		
to be a match for		
to meet one's match		

Then try matching the English ideas to the target-language words in the dictionaries. Can pupils make good use of the subheadings or categories in brackets? Or do they need to cross check the meaning by looking the word up in the target-language section?

The principle is the same as before. **If we take the time in the early years to make our pupils aware of possible pitfalls, we help them learn to avoid them.** In addition if we constantly make use of grammatical terminology, if we can help them see its usefulness, then, as the practice of checking or looking up words becomes part of class routine, they will need us less and less to emphasise the dangers and will be able more and more to rely on their own knowledge. They will learn to work independently.

Don't be surprised if your pupils still produce a few howlers! You may well come across misconceptions that you never dreamt of. Luckily all pupils' mistakes can be used by turning them round into exercises. A German friend whose pupils corresponded with mine, sent this extract back to me. It had taken her some time to work out what the writer's intention had been. I should add that we had spent a week in class learning and practising likes and dislikes before the letter was sent!

   '*Ich wie zu Schauspiel mein Rekord Spieler*'

A clear case of a pupil going home and not referring to what she had been learning, making no connection between what she wanted to say and what she had been taught. Instead she turned to a dictionary – and used it badly. She was also still at the stage of believing in the transliteration principle of one word in English: one word in German.

However well they may be copying and imitating and seemingly making use of new structures and words in class under our guidance, left to themselves they seem to slide back 'down the snake.' Free production seems to be able to bypass new language and fall back on language based on their mother tongue. It goes without saying that my next lesson began with a whole class exercise of looking up the word 'like' in the dictionary and finding out what the difference between a (vb) and an (adv) is and then referring back to the page in the coursebook we had just covered!

(Explanation: '*Ich* = I; *wie* = like, as (adv); *zu* = to (redundant here in German); *Schauspiel* = play, piece of theatre (noun); *mein* = my; *Rekord* = record, best time; *Spieler* = player.)

Constant practice

Dictionary work can easily become one of the regular starters at the beginning of lessons. If the focus of the exercise has immediate relevance and can be put into practice instantly, then all the better. The exercises can be explicit or implicit depending on how you wish to tackle these matters.

Exercises can be very simple

	m ou f?	le, la ou l'?	un ou une	mon ou ma?
appartement				
maison				
gîte				

	noun? substantif?	adjective? adjectif?	verb? verbe?	adverb? adverbe?
flat				
house				
garden				
well				
flower				

or can require much more investigation and thought.

It is essential that our pupils have an understanding of the different functions of words, the relevance of spelling and multiple meaning, of abbreviation and elision if they are to avoid common pitfalls, when they try to produce new language by themselves.

Structures are important ...

If Ringbom's theory 'that beginners will expect the target language to behave as their own with just lexical items being different' is sustainable, we should be able to predict this kind of behaviour – transliteration – in our pupils. In addition, we should expect them to fall into linguistic traps – more or less on a sliding scale depending on how much direct and explicit teaching of language they have received, before beginning their first foreign language.

How are we to help our pupils avoid transliteration? Or at least – if transliteration is a natural step in foreign language learning – how do we accelerate their progress through this stage so that they come out quickly on the other side with the lesson well learnt?

Once again Fredrich Bodmer shows the way. As long ago as 1944 he was advocating the triple translation technique; the target language, the transliteration, the English.

Je les ai vues à l'école
(I them have seen to the school)
I saw them at school

Ich habe sie in der Schule gesehen
(I have them in the school seen)
I saw them at school

Los vi en el colegio
(Them saw in the school)
I saw them at school

I have always used this system myself in the belief that if pupils understand the value of each separate unit of a phrase, they can quickly learn to transfer these elements to create new but similar structures. It also has the benefit of using transliteration but clearly not stopping there. **If pupils are naturally going to treat the foreign language in the same way as their own, with only a change of words, then we need to take this misconception and move it very deliberately and positively one step further to arrive at the right solution.**

So, from the beginning, phrases such as *Je m'appelle* are introduced as meaning 'I myself call' and the English meaning is given as either 'I'm ...' or 'My name is ...' or 'I'm called ... .'

The implicit lesson being learnt here is twofold: one – that the French and English structures are different and: two – English often offers a variety of phrases, all of which equally well address one single target-language idea or concept.

... so are functions

There is yet another important message to get across:

Our pupils until recently were not required to analyse the **function** of the words and structures they use in English. As a result many are still totally unaware, for example, that 'bigger' and 'more beautiful' share the same function – that they are both comparative forms. Because the two forms look different, pupils do not expect them to have any connection and so it will not occur to them to look for it. They will also expect to translate them differently into the target language. Similarly, they find it hard to grasp that four different ways of saying walk – I walk, I do walk, I am walking and I have been walking – can all be equally valid ways of indicating the Present Tense of a verb.

In the target language they have to understand that same concepts are realised by same forms: so 'bigger' and 'more beautiful' will have the same construction: '*plus grand*', '*plus beau*'; '*größer*', '*schöner*'; '*más grande*', '*más bonito*'. At some stage, they have to discover for themselves, or have revealed to them, that all four forms of any English Present Tense serve one function and so will be translated by a single form in the target language: '*je vais*', '*ich gehe*', '*voy*'.

The three-stage or triple translation technique can direct their attention to the frequency of similarities and dissimilarities between the mother tongue and the target language. And it is not a system the pupils find at all difficult. In class I have often overheard pupils, working in a group, use the triple translation and so avoid staying put at the transliteration stage.

'*Le grand chien noir* ... what's that? the ... big ... dog ... black ...Ah ha ... The big black dog.'

'Doesn't 'go' have to go to the end? I must today in the town go. That's what it has to be.'

'*Il me la donne samedi matin* … Hum? He … me … the … meaning 'it … from a '*la*' word … gives … Saturday morning. Hummm … He gives me it on Saturday morning? … What about: He'll give me it on Saturday morning … that makes more sense here.'

It is at moments like this when what you have taught comes boomeranging back and you know you have given them vital 'tags' in their recall system, 'tags' that stimulate the processes of locating internal information and then internal checking. **By deliberately using transliteration as an intermediate stage, we train them not to expect it to be the final stage.** By translating one word for one word, pupils can hear and see for themselves the false English that that process creates. Their common sense and their feeling for their own language will prompt them to offer other suggestions and in the process they become aware that, for example, a French Present Tense may be used to convey something we might use a Future Tense for.

This common sense and feel for language is evident in what the pupils say as they play around with words out loud. But it can also appear as a silent reaction. If I see children write something and then look silently at it, I congratulate them. 'What for?' they ask.' I haven't done anything. I was just looking at what I'd written.' 'Precisely!' I tell them. 'Well done! Giving your brain a chance to check it … excellent!'

What I hope, what I am sure, is going on inside, is an internal aural or visual check. We should be encouraging this covert activity openly – even though that sounds like a contradiction in terms!

6   What grammar means to us

One of the most frequent complaints I heard over the last two decades as an INSET provider was that MFL teachers felt that they had two roles to play: to teach the foreign language and to teach English grammar; many felt that without a knowledge of their own language it was difficult for pupils to proceed beyond the initial stages of foreign language learning.

The National Literacy Strategy (NLS), which has now been part of primary teaching since September 1998, and the Key Stage 3 Strategy which has been in place since 2002 are removing the 'burden' of grammar teaching from our shoulders and are helping to prepare pupils for foreign language learning.

There have been various reports over the last few decades (Bullock, Kingman, Cox) focusing on the importance of looking at language across the curriculum. All have agreed that there should be no return to the kind of grammar teaching seen in the 50s and before. But at the same time they have pressed hard for recognition of the fact that knowledge of one's own language and the ability to talk about language can only enhance standards. They have emphasised that delivery is all important; so long as grammar is tackled in ways suitable to the understanding of the pupils being taught, then there can be nothing but advantage to be gained. It is precisely this that the NLS has been devised and designed to address.

No one is advocating a return to the dull days of parsing: but being able to analyse the function of a word is an essential skill, if sense is to be made of the myriad homographs and homophones that litter English. The pupil, who is unaware that 'me' is being used emphatically in the phrase 'It's only me!' but as a direct object in the phrase 'He sees me' and as an indirect object in the phrase 'he gives me the book', will make little sense of what is encountered in German, where all three functions will be served by a different form.

No one is suggesting mindless rote learning: but there may be an argument for mindful rote learning. In fact for some areas rote learning may prove yet to be a very functional learning strategy.

No one is disagreeing that 'visual and aural demonstrations that require an active response' as recommended by the MFL National Curriculum Working Party, can and do make a more vivid and lasting impact than a wordy explanation delivered in a monotone without any reference to context.

The following chapters offer ideas for active grammar learning. No one single way of dealing with grammar will be suggested; rather a range of ideas arising from evidence provided either by pupil error or by research findings should provide enough material for teachers to select those that suit their own method of teaching and the pupils they teach.

Those grammatical aspects which are absent in English have been concentrated on, not merely because to cover everything grammatical would be too extensive, but also because some of the latest neurological research has revealed that new knowledge requires the creation of new neural pathways in the brain. Activities that can accelerate their creation are suggested, some of which can be adapted time and again to suit different contexts: others are designed for one purpose only.

In 1989 Kate Beeching said:

'Grammar is the best core knowledge you can have of a language'

Now that we have cross-phase and cross-curriculum agreement on this, we no longer need to apologise for a focus on grammar, instead we have it as a core element, in all our teaching. Grammar consists of two main features: form (morphology) and structure (syntax). Both of these are rooted in fixed, recurring patterns. It is these patterns that pupils have to become familiar with, recognising their value and purpose and then making use of the same patterns, whether explicitly or not, to express their own ideas. Form must always be covered before structure; form comprises the bricks out of which structures will be built.

The concept of grammar

It is a strange fact that the further back in time you trace the European languages, the more strictly grammatical patterns apply. Our ancestors 2,000 or 20,000 years ago would not have tolerated such 'sloppiness' in their language as the homographs and homophones listed earlier. Nor would they have been happy with invariable forms to serve different functions. To them a noun had to sound like a noun and had somehow to indicate clearly whether it was the subject of a sentence or the object or the indirect object or being used prepositionally. An adjective had to show clearly which noun it was attached to; it could never have been mistaken for an adverb. But then in those days they did not have strict rules about word order. If words can be put in any order, then so many of the characteristics of the languages our ancestors developed for themselves make sense.

A number of words strung one after the other with no apparent connection cannot be understood. Context might on reflection give the meaning, but language has to work faster than that. There might not be time to think.

small big cave bear black dark in lives

Which cave? The small one or the big one? The black one or the dark one? And is it the cave that is big? Or the bear?

But if the words have some pattern to them that clearly links them, whatever their position, at least their relationship is clearer.

caveX darkY blackX bearY bigY inX smallX livesY

English relies almost entirely on linear word order and proximity to make relationships clear.

The big dark bear lives in the small black cave.

No one ever sat down and dictated the grammar of a language. It evolved with the people, satisfying their particular needs for communication and the way in which they wished to express themselves.

THE PERSPECTIVE OF THOUGHT

It is not just a case of sounding different but a matter of thinking differently. The thinking is different because each language lays greater or lesser importance on different salient features in the ideas its people are trying to communicate. I call these perspectives of thought and from them come the grammatical differences which shape individual languages.

The universality of language is what unites all human beings across the globe. The different perspectives of thought is what differentiates our languages.

Look at this picture, where the four separate images that comprise this idea are:

1 John the giver
2 the act of giving
3 what is being given
4 the person to whom it is being given

are seen in that order.

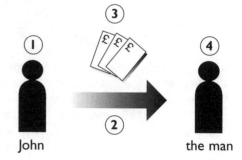

John   the man

When the French wish to convey this thought, they have to say:

Jean donne l'argent à l'homme. That is 1 + 2 + 3 + à + 4

The Germans, however, would see it differently:

Johann gibt dem Mann das Geld. That is 1 + 2 + 4 + 3

For the Germans the perspective changes and our mind having first taken in John as the giver (1), secondly the act of giving (2), then sees the person to whom it is being given as the next important piece of information (4); what is being given comes last (3). The images that comprise the idea are being seen in a different order from the French. What is more German does not need to include a preposition.

Because English has both these languages as parents, it should come as no surprise that we can use both patterns. We have decided to keep both perspectives, so we can say:

John gives the money to the man.   French perspective 1 + 2 + 3 + to + 4

or

John gives the man the money.   German perspective 1 + 2 + 4 + 3

But if we wish to communicate the same idea using pronouns, the perspectives change quite dramatically.

The French now see 1) the giver, then 3) the object given, then 4) the person to whom it is given and finally 2) the act of giving.

Jean donne l'argent à l'homme.   *Jean le lui donne.*   1 + 3 + 4 + 2

The Germans also change the order. Now they prefer placing the object given before the person to whom it is being given. To do this they have to reverse the previous order.

Johann gibt dem Mann das Geld.   *Johann gibt es ihm.*   1 + 2 + 3 + 4

And the English? Well the English say – why bother changing a couple of good perspectives! It makes no changes at all and retains the noun word order exactly.

John gives the money to the man.   John gives the man the money.
John gives it to him.   John gives him it.
1 + 2 + 3 + to + 4   1 + 2 + 4 + 3

Grammar, as found in coursebooks or grammar books, is a way of codifying in words and examples all these perspectives. In order to learn another language, we need to understand its perspectives of thought and the characteristics of the individual images that comprise those thoughts. We can very often understand these best by 'seeing' the concept at work in our mind's eye, by imagining the whole idea as a series of individual images and noting how and when their perspective or an individual characteristic differs from ours. Once we can do this, we have a language's grammar.

It will help if we can put ourselves in the linguistic shoes of the target language and find, not only differences between their perspectives and ours, but perhaps also even reasons for them.

THE LOGIC OF FRENCH ADJECTIVES

When introducing French adjectives, I tell the pupils that, except for a limited number, all adjectives will follow the noun. That the French say 'a house white, my bike green, my small dog black, etc'. Someone in the class usually makes the comment 'how silly' or words to that effect. I immediately pick up this comment and turn it back to the class. 'Is it silly? Listen carefully, because what I am going to say is very, very important. At the end of this lesson I am going to give each and every one of you a red ... soft ... furry ... round ... Uhhhhhh!' and I collapse dramatically across the table without finishing the sentence!

'What am I going to give you?' I ask on immediately resurrecting myself.

'Something furry', 'A round red thing something', 'It was soft and furry' come the answers. 'You didn't get round to saying!' someone will remark.

'And that was English adjective word order, adjectives in a string and then at the end the noun, the item being described. Now listen again but this time I'll use the French system. At the end of this lesson I am going to give each and every one of you a cushion, soft, furry, round, red. You probably don't want it ... but at least you know this time what you're getting. Which way is clearer? And why?'

What follows is a simple straightforward language activity and discussion. By the end of it, the pupils will be freely admitting that the French is a better system. That you can't begin to picture the English idea until you get to the noun or item. As they were listening, they were all seeing different objects in their mind's eye. Whereas with the French system, you say the item/noun first and then describe it. This is easy to follow, changing the image as the adjectives are heard.

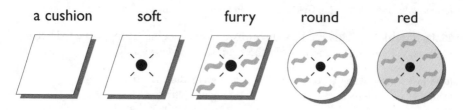

| a cushion | soft | furry | round | red |

This kind of reasoning can work just as well with concepts that do not even occur in our language. So you can introduce new concepts as well as re-order existing ones and ask pupils to judge them.

THE ACCURACY OF CASE ENDINGS

In order to introduce the concept of cases in German, I play on their usefulness. On the board I draw three pots sherds, one of which has 'the man' written on it, another 'the dog' and the third one 'bit'. And I ask the class to imagine that they are archaeologists who have discovered these three bits which obviously come from the same piece of pottery. 'What was the original sentence?'

The immediate response is 'The dog bit the man', though the chief joker in the class very often offers 'The man bit the dog'. If this happens, I nod and congratulate him or her – to their surprise – and point out that probability is not the same thing as possibility. Both sentences are possible. Only one is probable.

I then draw three more sherds. On these are written:

Der Mann   den Hund   biß.

This time they have to be German archaeologists, but before they make up their minds they have to know that '*der*' indicates the person/thing doing the action and '*den*' the person or thing it is being done to. 'Now what was the original sentence?'

And of course there is only one solution. 'The man bit the dog.'

'What would you have to say for it to mean the other way round?'

'*Der ... Hund biß ... den ... Mann.*'

'Correct! And which is the more reliable system? Which is the clearer? Which is unequivocal, i.e. can't be mistaken for anything else, has only one meaning?'

By offering reasons and simple demonstrations which all can understand, the obstacle of learning a new concept is reduced, if not removed. The learning to apply will still take time, but the bafflement caused by coming across a new concept is minimised.

Because we all share the ability to think in ideas and images, thought pictures and their perspectives can be one way of approaching the larger grammatical dimension. Having understood the concept, however, there is still the realisation of each individual image into foreign words and this can sometimes call for new procedures of storage and recall.

DEALING WITH GENDER AND GENDER AGREEMENT

The definite article in English is 'the' – an invariable. It can be followed by an adjective, also invariable in form. Any adjective can be reused as it is read, as it is heard or as given in a dictionary; there is no need to consider any agreements or positioning. It can be used as found: 'the big ...', 'the small ...', 'the red ... .'

For any French or German student learning English this must seem a gift. The six forms for 'the' in German used in sixteen different ways are reduced to one: for the French and Spanish, four forms are reduced to one. From the first lesson on, they can be reassured that they are going to be accurate in simple description. There are no choices to be made: 'the large ..., the small ..., the old.' They even have the time to consider what noun to use and still know that they are correct in what they are saying: 'the black ... dog', 'the black ... book', 'the black ... elephant.'

They have one more linguistic luxury; they can wait (for most nouns at least) until the very end of articulating the noun before deciding whether to make it plural or not: 'the black ... dogs', 'the black ... books', 'the black ... elephants'. This lineality of thought is uniquely English among European languages, as is the lack of gender and agreement.

In order to achieve the same in German, French or Spanish the English speaking brain has to be trained to gather its information in a totally different way. For a start it has to begin at the opposite end considering first whether a word is plural or not. Here is the procedure of analysis that has to take place somewhere in the brain in order to produce 'the' in French.

To produce 'the' in French.

Step 1 Is the noun singular of plural? If plural, use '*les*'.
Step 2 If singular, does it start with a vowel? If yes, use '*l'*'.
Step 3 If not, then it is either '*le*' or '*la*' – Either you will have learnt this or you will have to check in the dictionary.

PS. You can give up this last stage when you have guessed correctly five times on the trot before you get to the word in the dictionary!

Before an adjective can be added – 'the black book' – the gender of the noun to be used has to be known, as well as the position of the adjective. The choices are:

> *Le noir livre*
> *La noire livre*
> *Le livre noir*
> *La livre noire*

Or any other combination our pupils can come up with!

And if they want to talk about black books in the plural, they cannot wait until the end and add an 's': they have to add this into the calculation from the beginning – for the article and the adjective as well as the noun!

So English-speaking learners of French have to pinpoint the noun and its number and gender first and then work through a procedure of choices, before a simple description using a definite article, an adjective and a noun, whether singular or plural, can be produced. And their confidence in being accurate at each stage of choice will never match that of their European peers, who can blithely put together from their first lesson onwards: 'The open door', 'The small chair', 'The red coat', etc.

Small wonder, then, that our pupils find the learning of a foreign language such hard work compared to the relatively easy experience their European counterparts have when learning English – at least in the initial stages.

The procedure illustrated above plays on cognitive skills which we already possess. We do have a system for choosing between two forms – 'this' and 'these': 'that' and 'those'. So choice between singular and plural is already something we recognise. We also have a system for changing a word if the following word begins with a vowel: 'a pear' but 'an apple'. So checking for nouns with initial vowels is not unknown to us. So why not make use of these existing systems to create a new one to cope with the French?

This procedure can become part and parcel of routine classwork during the early learning period. **If it is repeated often enough as a conscious procedure, it will eventually become an internal process, which will then become an automatic routine**. The brain will have been given a definite route of thought to lay down as a neural pathway, which it can then follow in order to retrieve the information required. Pupils often balk at Step 3 'checking gender in a dictionary'. But they should be encouraged by being told that it doesn't last for ever; you could even run a class competition on who can allocate the most correct genders without checking! Heats could be run every term and class champions could then be matched against their peers in other classes within the Year.

Spanish works just as easily with a similarly procedure. Unfortunately it is not as simple for German; here it is vital to know in advance, before analysis can begin, not just the gender of the noun, its number but also its use in the sentence. Function rears its important head – an understanding of even the most basic sentence analysis is required. Is it the subject? The direct object? The indirect object?

MAKE ROTE LEARNING ACTIVE

V. J. Cook in his essay 'Second language learning' (1982) concluded:

> *Above all the teacher should recognise the active contribution made by the learner; regardless of what the teacher wants him (sic) to do, the learner adopts certain learning and production strategies; success in learning is a product of many different factors in the learner, most of them out of the teacher's control.*

In order to bring some of these more under the control of the teacher, I turn to the computer again. Previously it has been suggested in Chapter 4 that the computer can make a unique contribution to learning because of its ability to monitor step by step pupils' own thinking, correcting and redirecting wrong thought procedures. I am now going to suggest another area in which the computer can contribute.

Teachers traditionally trained pupils to learn by heart sets of information, such as the learning of mathematical tables, special spellings such as "'i' before 'e' except after 'c'" and in MFL teaching the creation of regular verbs 'Take off the -er and add -e, -es -e, -ons, -ez, -ent' by making them repeat them over and over again. Neuroscience research is now discovering that rote learning, as it was called, had positive benefits; it created the necessary cognitive pathways for fixing and recalling information. Despite the fact that it has been discredited by many educational pedagogues for a long time, many MFL teachers have continued to encourage their pupils to learn by rote: for example the formation of past participles in French, the main parts of the verb in German. For pupils who are academic, these verbal directions are enough. They can take them into their brain and, with a bit of practice, apply them for ever more. But for the greater majority, they remain like distant commandments; pupils know they should follow them but, in the hurly burly of reality, forget to do so.

If, however, the verbal repetition can be converted into a real activity, then the storing and recalling processes of the mind get yet another chance at learning. Using a word processor and its facilities to delete, insert and move, many of the individual grammatical points can be turned into graphic reality. When we demonstrate that French pronouns come in front of the verb, for example, let your pupils actually watch you move them in front using Highlight and Drag in Word on an electronic whiteboard; then ask a few pupils up to the board to imitate your actions; follow this up in the next MFL ICT lesson with individual work. Having seen the demonstration, having watched some colleagues following the same steps, most pupils will be able to work through a similar file on their own with a minimum of guidance.

> *Experience sculptures the brain through patterns of connections. After a few repetitions of cell groups firing together they tend to team up. This is called Hebbian learning after the Canadian psychologist Donald Hebb. When two connected neurones have been triggered together on several occasions the cells and synapses between them change chemically so that when one fires it will be a stronger trigger to the other.* (Winkley 1999)

The connection is made and is being made more secure each time the experience is repeated.

> *Perhaps the key point to draw from all this is that the brain is like a muscle and develops through use: if mental processes and thinking strategies which originate in neural pathways are not developed and used, the inevitable result is that the brain cells will die and the potential will be lost.*

> *Activities including all kinds of learning and cognitive memory are dependent on the neural network being activated, with the result that the more each network is activated and used, the more learning and memory will take place.* (ibid)

It's so simple, really. It is called activity dependent brain changes. Do something only once and you don't have much to remember it by. Do something over and over again and you build a neural pathway in the brain which strengthens every time you use it. The brain actually grows in density as the new information is laid down. Eventually the brain takes over and unbidden, unconsciously and automatically follows that pathway, whenever the same stimulus occurs.

This is learning: the biological organisation of new experience. And by making rote learning active and turning dry as dust verbal instructions into real actions, we can help pupils organise quickly efficiently and effectively new sets of information.

8   Dealing with gender

In the brain of an English-speaking language learner, who has never consciously encountered French or German or Spanish before, there are no neural networks ready and prepared to make sense of the stream of sound that will be heard from their first lesson onward. Pupils can only interpret what they see and hear through their previous experience of language. This means that grammatical items such as gender will have no relevance to them, unless we make it relevant from the start. And we need to be consistent in our approach and constant in its repetition.

EMPHASISING GENDER

In Marie Surridge's book '*Le ou la? The gender of French nouns*' she notes that French mothers tend not to talk to their babies just using an article and a noun. '*Voici une pomme! Voici une voiture! C'est un chien!*' Rather they invariably add one or more adjectives, which gives the baby a second bite of the 'gender cherry'. '*Voici une pomme verte! Voici une petite voiture blanche! C'est un grand chien noir!*'

This is something we can all do. As we introduce new vocabulary with our flashcards, why not add an adjective or two. Not only are we improving the gender element of the recall but we are also giving our pupils a more creative and dramatic word base. If they initially learn '*Une petite voiture blanche*' it is unlikely that they will recall just plain '*une voiture*', instead they will automatically recall '*une voiture blanche*' or '*une petite voiture*'.

USING COLOUR CODING

When making labels to support existing flashcards, agree with colleagues in the department a colour code for all languages being taught and print out one set of labels colour coded and another set in black. This is because at some point in the learning, you have to remove the prompts and let them use the clues of the words or articles themselves. But to start with, colour coding is useful.

GENDER WALLS

Some children are very spatially aware. This awareness can be harnessed to reinforce gender of new vocabulary by allocating one wall of the classroom to pictures/flashcards of masculine words and another to feminine words; obviously, a third wall is required for the neuter in German. As new words are introduced, their flashcards can be pinned up on the appropriate wall.

This will give you lots of extra possibilities for making sure gender is reinforced.

1   Having introduced and practised the new vocabulary in your usual way, hand out the flashcards to a group of pupils and ask them to sort them out onto the correct walls.

2   Check that they are in the right place by handing out the coloured labels to another group. If the flashcards have been placed correctly and the second group label them correctly, all the same coloured labels will be on one wall. Try it again with non-coloured labels.

3   Before the pupils come into the classroom, pin up flashcards randomly in the two/three gender areas. How quickly can a group of pupils sort them back into their correct places?

4   Take the flashcards away. Call out the vocabulary and pupils have to point to the correct gender wall.

You can hang posters with an ever-increasing list of articles, possessives, etc, on the same wall too. This will allow pupils to put articles together with, not just the nouns that are still on the wall, but also the vocabulary of previous units, such is the spatial recall of some pupils.

le	la		les
un	une		des
mon	ma	and on both	mes
ton	ta	walls the	tes
son	sa	plural	ses
notre	notre		nos
votre	votre		vos
leur	leur		leurs
ce	cette		ces
ce ... ci	cette ... ci		ceux-ci
ce ... là	cette ... là		ceux-là

Adjective forms can also be pinned up.

The benefits of this system remain with some pupils throughout the five years:

'I always remember that word. It was just over my friend's shoulder ... on the wall behind her ... Every time I looked at her, I saw it. I can still see it.'

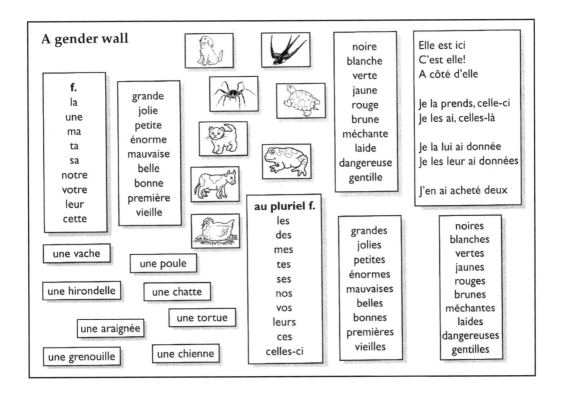

A gender wall

f.	grande			noire	Elle est ici
la	jolie			blanche	C'est elle!
une	petite			verte	A côté d'elle
ma	énorme			jaune	
ta	mauvaise			rouge	Je la prends, celle-ci
sa	belle			brune	Je les ai, celles-là
notre	bonne			méchante	
votre	première			laide	Je la lui ai donnée
leur	vieille			dangereuse	Je les leur ai données
cette				gentille	

une vache

une poule

une hirondelle

une chatte

une araignée

une tortue

une grenouille

une chienne

au pluriel f.

les
des
mes
tes
ses
nos
vos
leurs
ces
celles-ci

J'en ai acheté deux

grandes	noires
jolies	blanches
petites	vertes
énormes	jaunes
mauvaises	rouges
belles	brunes
bonnes	méchantes
premières	laides
vieilles	dangereuses
	gentilles

'To remember whether it's a 'le' or 'la' word I just think … did I see it up there on the right or the left? If I can 'see' it on the left, then I know it's 'le".

THE GENDER DIVIDE

If you are unfortunate to have a classroom that is more glass than walls, you may not be able to use the gender walls idea. An alternative is to divide one wall into several sections and use the far left and far right sections as the two gender areas – with a central one being employed as well in the case of German.

Or you could divide the class itself into 2–3 gender groups. As new words are being learnt, hand the flashcards to the appropriate group. Next lesson can the class remember which flashcards belong to which gender group? When gender agreements are being taught, get each gender group to learn theirs. They then become 'the class experts' for that information. Then when practising and doing exercises, you can point to the correct gender group to elicit the correct form.

STORING GENDER I

Research done in Canada by André Rigault revealed that the French appear to retrieve gender aurally, that the pattern of sound made by a word suggests which gender it is likely to be.

To encourage and develop similar skills, brief listening exercises should be included regularly as starter activities right from the beginning, in which pupils listen to words and have to write them down in the correct column headed – 'le' or 'la' or 'der', 'die' or 'das' or hold up appropriate cards that are colour coded or just hold up the right or left hand.

The aim is to train the internal aural recall of our pupils by repeatedly requiring the brain to check internally for what sounds like the correct gender and to give immediate feedback as to the correct answer.

STORING GENDER 2

Take a leaf out of CILT's Young Pathfinder 8: *Grammar is fun* (Biriotti 1999), where it is suggested that you take all the unit vocabulary of one gender and build the words into a story in English. Then repeat the activity with vocabulary of the other gender/s. The association techniques of the brain will do the rest! Once you have demonstrated this technique to pupils, encourage them to use it as an easy way of storing gender, whenever they learn new vocabulary.

For example:

Camarades 2, Unit 3: *Une invitée idéale?* (Pillette 1997, Nelson Thornes)

'*Le*' words

Last **weekend** I wanted to go **bowling** with my friend. I was staying over, so I packed my **bag**: **jumper, trainers**, etc. 'Don't forget your **money**, said Mum. 'and you'd better pack some **shampoo, soap** … oh and your **toothpaste** in case you have a **bath** … Now what's the **problem**?' I had lost my **wallet**. 'It's with the **umbrella** in the **hall**. Have you done all your **homework**? No? Are you taking your **exercise book** so you can finish?

'*La* words'

When I got back from the **skating rink** yesterday I had a **shower** and a drink of **lemonade**. I was going to the **disco** later, but I couldn't find my **toothbrush**. I looked everywhere and eventually found it in my **pencil case**! Mum had already paid for my **entrance** over the internet by **Visacard**. Thanks Mum!

 GENDER DRAG

When using linear wordsearches as an ICT activity – a starter to a computer lesson perhaps – ask pupils once the words have been cut out, to highlight and drag the words into the correct gender column of the table beneath. As knowledge progresses, the gender could be indicated by possessives, demonstratives or grammatically inflected forms such as *au/à la //aux* or *dem/der//den*.

brückerathausschulefreibadkonzerthallebahnhofhäusernapothekebuchhandlungsupermarkt

zum	zur	zum	zu den
Marktplatz	Kirche	Kino	Geschäften

chevalserpenthamstergerbillesescargotcochond'Indearaignée

Mon petit	Ma petite	Mes petits	Mes petites
chien	perruche	poissons	
chat			
oiseau			

CHECKING GENDER

The idea of using a dictionary to check gender can be used to create an exercise for pairwork.

- Each pupil writes down any six words from the current topic with what they believe to be the correct gender.
- The list is then passed to the partner for checking.
- First of all the partner ticks the words he or she believes to be right and crosses the words he or she thinks have been given the wrong gender.
- He or she then checks in a dictionary/glossary and in the second column ticks or crosses whether the original entry was correct or not.

There will be two results: pupil 1 may have got 5/6 right and pupil 2 may have spotted the mistake and so gets 6/6.

The marker's score is calculated by the number of matching X's and ✓'s in the two columns.

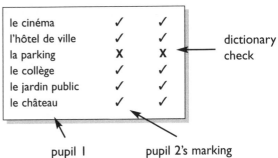

le cinéma	✓	✓	
l'hôtel de ville	✓	✓	dictionary
la parking	X	X	check
le collège	✓	✓	
le jardin public	✓	✓	
le château	✓	✓	

pupil 1   pupil 2's marking

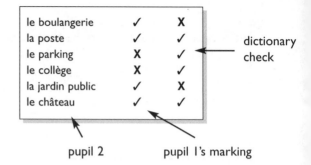

le boulangerie	✓	X
la poste	✓	✓
le parking	X	✓
le collège	X	✓
la jardin public	✓	X
le château	✓	✓

dictionary check

pupil 2   pupil 1's marking

Pupil 2 may have got 4/6 right and pupil 1 may have considered two of those wrong, when in fact they were right and did not spot either of the other two, leaving him or her with a score of just 2/6.

There are only two matching symbols in the two columns, so pupil 1 scores only two points, whereas four of the original entries were correct, so pupil 2 gets 4/6.

A simpler version of this exercise makes a useful starter activity, as it needs no preparation. Pupils work in pairs:

- Each of the two pupils writes a list of six to eight words learnt recently. The list should be in English.
- They then swap lists and have to give the gender and target-language word for each word on the other's list. They then hand the paper back to their partner.
- The trick is that each pupil must be able to correct the other's effort, i.e. has got to know the answer themselves … or check if there is any dispute.
- The articles to be added do not have to be the definite article: as they are learnt, a point could be made of adding indefinites, possessives, demonstratives.

ICT AND GENDER

For these kind of activities you need either an authoring program or you can just use Word. The only problem with using the latter is that it will not check the pupils' work; you will have to do that for them either as they go along or at the end.

GAPKIT (Camsoft) allows teachers to author text and gap whole words or parts of words. So it is easy to create a file where the article is gapped and has to be filled in by the pupil. Pupils will be allowed a second go at the ones they get wrong. They can re-start the exercise as many times as they like, until they are able to get a perfect score. Follow it up with an exercise where the English word is not gapped but the target-language word is, both article and noun … an electronic vocabulary test!

Don't just use this kind of exercise when initially learning vocabulary; it is just as valuable when reinforcing grammatical inflection too:

[du] pain	*[de la] limonade*	*[de l'] eau*	*[des] petits pains*
Der große Hund	*Die kleine Katze*	*das alte Pferd*	*die neuen Fische*
[ein großer] Hund	*[eine kleine] Katze*	*[ein altes] Pferd*	*[neue] Fische*
[el] dibujo	*[la] geografía*	*[los] trabajos manuals*	*[las] matemáticas*

If you can find an authoring program that includes a sentence sequencer, where individual words can be dragged into their proper order, then you can create exercises like the following where the pupils have to restore the pair of nouns with their correct articles and adjectives. Not easy! They will be hopeless at first but let them persevere and they will develop strategies to deal with such demands.

petite et brune chien une Un brun souris petit

These can also be created in WORD but there is obviously no way of checking the results. That's OK in an ICT lesson as you are free to walk around and observe pupils as they work. You can help them initially by randomly calling out the correct answers '*Un petit chien brun et une petite souris brune*', '*Une poisson rouge et des oiseaux verts*', '*Un grand cheval noir et une grande tortue noire*'. Their short term memories will hold the sound of the answers until they need them. On their second and third goes you will see them digging ever deeper into their memories as the correct answers embed themselves.

(For more detailed analysis on the benefits of sequencing see CILT's *Reflections on ICT* (Atkinson 2001), 'Developing a sense of gender in French'.)

I was once checking various exam criteria with a GCSE examiner. I asked her how much importance in the oral exam was laid on wrong gender. 'If a candidate said '*un personne*' and not '*une personne*', for example, would that count as a minor error or a serious error?' In the other corner of the room, a colleague, who was French, put her hands to her ears and shuddered. Interested in her reaction, I asked what was wrong. She replied that listening as she had been with half an ear, the sound of '*un personne*' had not registered with her as a mistake for '*une personne*'. Rather her brain had instantly started filtering through other possibilities as alternatives to the sound '*un*' in relationship to '*personne*'. It had come up with '*vingt*' before the rest of the sentence had arrested her attempt and she had realised what her ears had led her brain to do.

Surridge gives a similar example to highlight the importance of gender to the 'sympathetic native speaker' – the audience for all GCSE efforts.

> *To the learner, a gender error seems like a tiny and unimportant mistake which will not affect the sense of the utterance. Yet if you look closely at the reactions of Francophones to such mistakes, you will realise that the result is often total incomprehension. Try asking for* 'une petite pain'. *The listener may realise that you have made a gender error or, on the other hand, wonder what you mean by* 'pain' *which, since you made it feminine, simply cannot mean 'bread', 'roll' or 'bun'.*
> (Surridge 1995)

Gender is more than a definite or indefinite article: it is all the patterns tied to a single noun: the possessives adjectives; the demonstratives; the pronouns; the adjective agreements. It is not enough to allow pupils to develop their own ideas of what gender a noun should be. Nor should they be taught some universal sound, like the Homer Simpson style 'Doh' as one German teacher told me she does in the hope that sloppiness of speech will disguise the fact that the grammar is lacking. Far better that time is spent in those vital, habit-forming years giving them the chance to build a solid base on which to build the learning of later years.

9 Structure

Structure comprises the ways in which words are strung together, i.e. the order in which concepts are presented in words.

It can be:

Subject verb Object (linear)   or not (non linear)

I see him   *Ich sehe ihn*   but   *je **le** vois*

It can require the splitting of a concept into more than one word and the placing of each word in a non-linear sequence.

*Je **ne** les ai **pas** vus*   *Wir **stiegen** in Bonn **aus***   He **took** his coat **off**

It can have more than one possible sequence.

I saw the man every day on the bus.

i)   *Ich sah den Mann jeden Tag auf dem Bus.*
ii) *Jeden Tag sah ich den Mann auf dem Bus.*
iii) *Den Mann sah ich jeden Tag auf dem Bus.*

It can change its purpose with a difference of intonation which will be marked in writing by punctuation.

You bought the car.   You bought the car!
You bought **the car**? **You** bought the car?   You **bought** the car?

In English, you can start a sentence without necessarily knowing exactly what is going to be said and can deviate into new ideas quite happily.

As I was … running down the … stairs this … afternoon, I … fell over … my little brown … hat and squashed it. So I'm afraid you can't borrow it.

As I was … saying, before the … boy interrupted us, I would be more than happy to … lend you … my hat.

It is perfectly possible to redirect the sentences above at every series of dots:

As I was … eating my meal … As I was … saying before the … bell rang.

It is impossible to do this in the languages most often taught in British schools: they must have a clear idea of the whole sentence before they start. This is new to our way of thinking and so will be the ways in which the respective target languages build their sentences.

> *Our research findings suggest that a child's speech becomes creative through the gradual analyses of the internal structure of sequences which begin as prepackaged routines.* (Clark 1974)

> *One assumption that is widely held as axiomatic is that people learn by doing. We seem to have deduced that people learn to speak by speaking and so on. In reality one simply drowns by attempting to swim without some sort of prior preparation and theoretical instruction.* (Walls 1992)

So prepackaged routines and prior preparation are the first steps: the next steps are manipulating them according to set patterns: and then finally using them as models to express our own ideas and thoughts.

Unfortunately the GCSE syllabus has been criticised for the lack of opportunity to do just this. There are prepackaged routines aplenty: but the minimal amount of manipulation that limited lesson-time allows them, rarely pushes any pupils other than the very brightest onto the next step and then on to the creative use of language.

But of course that is exactly what we should be doing; helping and encouraging our pupils up and over the steps. It is only once they experience being able to use even a small amount of language for themselves that the excitement generated by expressing one's own thoughts in a language other than one's mother tongue will be felt.

Perhaps the solution is to jump over the first step and, if not avoid it all together, at least minimise the number of fixed routines we ask them to learn by heart. After all, as Chris Brumfit (1980) said:

> *We are not teaching a limited set of behaviours but a capacity to produce those behaviours.*

If we support more the use of prefabricated patterns rather than prefabricated fixed routines, we will be offering our pupils choice in how they express themselves, which is surely nearer creativity and independence.

USING LITTLE BITS OF PAPER

If we want our pupils to move off the plateau of National Curriculum Level 4, they have to learn that there are X numbers of ways of expressing the same basic content in increasingly sophisticated ways. Which level of sophistication they decide to adopt, will be up to them but at least they will have had a range to choose from. The idea behind this kind of exercise is that pupils are given the content ideas and have to supply, first, the intonation and then the sentence pattern being learnt to complete the expression.

You will need to demonstrate this to the whole class before asking pupils to work in pairs or groups.

For example:

TV programmes

- Make one set of cards with the names of current TV programmes.
- Make one set of cards with single word expressions (opinions).
- Place the cards face down in their respective piles.

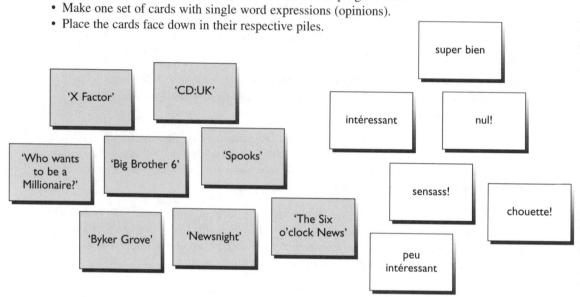

- Draw the top card from each pile and read the TV programme card as if it were a question, e.g. *'Newsnight'*?

- Read the opinion card with real meaning – and appropriate facial expression and gestures. *Sensass!!!*

- Repeat with the next two cards and then the next two. *'Spooks'? Chouette! 'X Factor'? Nul!*

- Return all six cards to the proper pile and invite a pupil to imitate what you have just done.

- Then ask the groups/pairs to do the same with their sets of cards.

Now repeat the demonstration but this time embed one or other in a suitable structure.

- *'Newsnight'? C'est ... pénible!*
- *'Byker Grove'? C'est ... sensass!*
- *'Big Brother'? C'est ... super bien!*

- *'Newsnight'? Je le trouve ... pénible!*
- *'Byker Grove'? Je le trouve ... sensass!*
- *'Big Brother'? Je le trouve ... super bien!*

Develop the exercise whenever appropriate by embedding the information in ever more complex structures.

- *J'aime … 'Spooks'. Je le trouve sensass!*
- *Je déteste 'Newsnight'. Je le trouve nul.*

(make sure both cards are drawn simultaneously so the correct j'aime/je déteste can be chosen)

The same exercise can be re-presented at a later date when tenses need to be practised.

- *Hier j'ai vu … 'CD:UK'. C'était … chouette!*
- *Hier j'ai vu … The 'Six o'clock News'. C'était … peu intéressant!*

There is no limit to the structures that can be practised with these same two simple piles of prompts.

- *Tu as vu … hier? C'était …*
- (pupils working in pairs; each takes one card) Pupil A: *Tu aimes …?* Pupil B: *Je le trouve …*
- *Est-ce que tu trouves … ?* (both prompts fitted into one structure)
- *Je n'ai jamais vu … On me dit que c'est …*
- *Ce que je pense de … ? Eh ben, moi, je le trouve …*

STRIPS

People in the media, whether broadcasters, journalists or actors, give a very false impression of 'speaking': they use full, well constructed sentences which pursue an argument or a line of questioning that clearly reveals its content. They produce seemingly off-the-cuff comment that is coherent and grammatical. Except – it is usually scripted either by them or for them; they may have to film many 'takes' before they get it just right. In fact they put a great deal of effort into making it appear natural!

Any Vox Pop, on the other hand, is much more revealing about how we express our thoughts in words. The replies from ordinary people caught 'on the hop' will be full of 'umms' and 'errs'; sentences will be started and not finished; ideas will get tangled and twisted around each other; references will be made to ideas thought but not uttered. What is most likely to be entirely missing are whole sentences, which are grammatically accurate and sequential.

And yet this is precisely the kind of dialogue we put in front of our pupils to learn off by heart! And then they, in their anxiety to please, become convinced that if they do not say it exactly as written, then they are **wrong**: for them it is not a matter of only half communicating ideas, the 'task' is to learn each and every word. Miss out one word or sound and they are flummoxed.

Language has its own progression – whichever language you look at. You can communicate quite successfully with a single word or two. A few more phrases gets you further. A string of linked ideas will extend any response and none of these need contain a finite verb at all!

'What's your favourite sport?'
'Football'.

'What do you do on Saturdays?'
'On Saturdays? Watch TV or go out with my friends'.

'How do you help at home?'
'Wash up, walk the dog … most days … mow the lawn … occasionally.

Rarely, if ever, would you hear anyone reply:

'My favourite sport is football'.
'On Saturdays I watch TV or I go out with my friends'.
'I wash up. Most days I walk the dog and I occasionally mow the lawn.'

This is written language spoken; it is not real spoken language.

Why do we make it difficult for our pupils? Why not start off teaching them the simplest of answers first, then over the next few terms or years extend into a chain of simple answers, vary it with a few time phrases and conjunctions and leave the difficult bit – working out the correct form of the finite verb – until the very last and then only demand it of those pupils who are likely to be able to cope.

To develop this kind of response I use Strips.

1	2	3	4	5	6
Tous les jours	le soir	j'aime	regarder la télé	et	regarder la télé
D'habitude	après le dîner	je préfère	lire	ou	lire
Si j'ai le temps	après le collège	je déteste	écouter des disques	et si possible	écouter des disques
Quand je peux	vers six heures	je n'aime pas	faire les devoirs		faire les devoirs
Si possible	après le devoirs	je dois	aller jouer au foot		aller jouer au foot
			écouter la radio		écouter la radio
			sortir avec des amis		sortir avec des amis
			faire du sport		faire du sport

At first I focus on column six and ask them to use it for their reply to the question:

Qu'est-ce que tu aimes faire comme passe-temps?

Encourage them to sound more natural by repeating the tail end of the question, making an 'ur umm' kind of sound as if they were reflecting on their answer, before adding something from column six with the slightest of pauses in-between.

Comme passe-temps? Bof! ... aller jouer au foot.
Comme passe-temps? Eh ben! ... sortir avec des amis.

Extend their reply by asking for something from columns 4, 5 and 6.

Comme passe-temps? Bof! ... aller jouer au foot et regarder la télé.
Comme passe-temps? Eh ben! ... sortir avec des amis ou écouter des disques.

When time phrases have been introduced, repeat the activity but extend it by asking for something from column 1 **or** column 2.

Comme passe-temps? Bof! ... si j'ai le temps ... aller jouer au foot et regarder la télé.
Comme passe-temps? Eh ben! ... d'habitude ... sortir avec des amis ou écouter des disques.

Extend by asking for something from column 1 **and** column 2.

Comme passe-temps? Bof! ... si j'ai le temps, après les devoirs ... aller jouer au foot et regarder la télé.
Comme passe-temps? Eh ben! ... d'habitude vers six heures ... sortir avec des amis ou écouter des disques.

And finally in Year 10 you can re-use the exercise again but this time add the verb from column 3.

Comme passe-temps? Eh ben! ... d'habitude vers six heures je préfère sortir avec des amis ou écouter des disques.

Once again, it is for them to decide at what stage of this extension they are going to stop in their individual learning. If GCSE oral marking still insists on full sentences, then strip 3 certainly needs to be added in Key Stage 4.

The extra advantage of this approach is that pupils can learn the greater part of their vocabulary of verbs as infinitives, i.e. as found in glossaries or dictionaries and use them either by themselves like this or in conjunction with a few 'tags' such as the modals: 'I want to', 'I can', 'I have to', 'I ought to' and others such as 'I like', 'I don't like', 'I hate', 'I can't stand'. Even fairly low ability pupils can cope with a future tense using *aller* + infinitive or a past tense using the concept: *je viens de* + infinitive. Although these two latter idioms do not exist in German it was pointed out by one German teacher that you can do a lot with *ich wollte, ich musste* for past tenses and a few future time phrases to add to the present tense verbs.

MANIPULATING THE PARTS

You can bring the structures to be taught alive by making them into individual word/phrase 'bricks', which pupils have to sort into order in front of the class.

Make a smaller set for yourself to demonstrate with first. These 'bricks' could be for the OHP or they could be A4 and large enough to stick on the board. Alternatively, if you have a white-board and projector, use highlight and drag of invidual words in Word.

Each brick has one element of a sentence or phrase on it.

- You move the cards into order.
- A pupil moves the cards into order.
- The class corrects the efforts of their colleague.

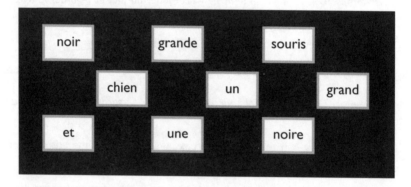

Next lesson have the A4 set handy and ask a group of pupils to do the same sorting exercise you did the previous lesson but this time in front of the class. I appoint one member of the group to be 'The organiser' who gives instructions to the rest of the group and arranges them and the card they each hold into the proper sequence. The rest of the class have to judge their efforts. Make enough bricks to create about 4–6 sentences.

If at all possible, develop this into a group or pairwork exercise by having sets of small 'bricks' for them to sort by themselves, along the lines of the Word Book used in primary schools, where pupils store the individual word cards they need to make basic sentences: they rearrange them into new sentences, which they copy into their exercises books. By playing around with their word/phrase bricks, pupils can experience, perhaps for the first time, that feeling of making language their own, by putting together new and original combinations.

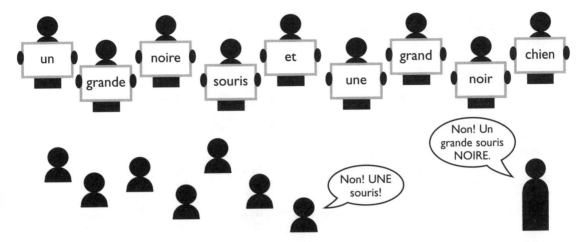

You can use the same technique of large word tiles to demonstrate new grammatical patterns, such as the French negative or German word order. It works very well for pronouns and changing articles to possessives or demonstratives. In these cases, where individual word/phrase elements are to be manipulated and changed, all you need do is print the words back to back.

1 Possessives

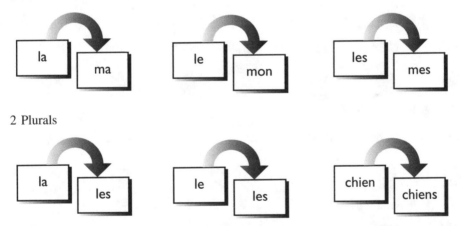

2 Plurals

The exercise can start quite simply; a pair of pupils stand at the front and you call out the first phrase, 'The dog'; the pupils pick up and hold out to the class the correct word tiles; you then call 'The dogs' and they have to turn over both tiles to make '*les chiens*' appear to the class. There has to be co-operation between the two pupils: they cannot work independently, which brings home implicitly the notion that the relationship between these two words is somewhat more than in English.

You can extend into adjectives

A/big/black/dog ⟶ Two/big/black/dogs

Such a display where all words must be turned to change to the plural form makes a visual impact, which if repeated often enough, will impress on the mind that the French say 'Two bigs dogs blacks.' This should aid recall immensely.

And then to full sentences.

I play with a dog. ⟶ I play with my dog.

I play with my dog. ⟶ I play with my dogs.

It is an excellent technique to use where word order has to change. Here pupils holding cards must be directed to a new position in the sequence – a very clear and obvious reminder of the difference in word order.

French negatives require one pupil to have two cards, which are then brought round on either side of the verb.

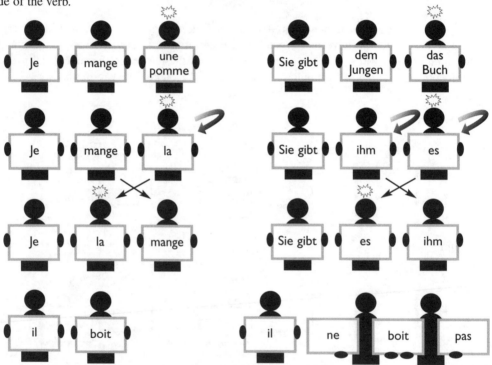

ICT AND STRUCTURES

The word-processing facilities of highlight and drag turn the manipulation of structures into an easy exercise. They allow us to demonstrate the transferability of like structures and then give pupils endless opportunities of mixing and matching sentences elements, either intentionally to create a specific meaning or randomly to see what they have made up. I call such exercises Dictate and Create, because in the first instance, the teacher dictates an

English sentence to be made up from the elements on offer: then the teacher hands over to the pupils to see what new sentences they can come up with. In addition, in the example below, pupils arrive at proper word order, just by selecting from one column after the other.

Dictate and Create file from *Just Click. Na klar! 1*
ICT Resource (Rendall 2006, Nelson Thornes)

> How would you say in German ... "I have to make the beds every morning?"

	meiner Mutter	ins Bett	
Du musst	jeden Nachmittag	deine Hausaufgaben	machen
Oma muss			ausräumen
	am Samstag morgen		einkaufen gehen
Meine Schwester muss	jeden Abend	die Spülmaschine	helfen
Mein kleiner Bruder muss	meinem Vater	im Garten	aufräumen
Wir müssen		in der Küche	
Meine Brüder müssen	das Wohnzimmer	direkt nach Hause	

1 Vati muss um 9 Uhr in die Stadt gehen.

2 Ich muss jeden Morgen die Betten

Obviously best done as an individual exercise, it is still effective, if time in the computer room is strictly limited, as a whole class exercise projected onto an ordinary whiteboard or an electronic whiteboard. We should be offering regular opportunities to manipulate and adapt sentences. Once this has become a regular feature of lessons, pupils will soon begin to develop a feel for the sentence structures they need.

It is also important to remember to translate any newly created sentences **a** so you know what they are supposed to mean and **b** so pupils can get a feeling for the worth of each element.

Example

Make your own sentences: translate each one into English underneath.

les enfants	voudrait	recycler	des journaux	pour gagner de l'argent
mon amie	voudraient	vendre	des bibelots	pour en avoir de la place
mes parents	pourrait	se débarrasser	la maison	pour être plus cool
ma sœur	pourraient	acheter	des vêtements	pour être plus à la mode

1 Les enfants voudraient vendre des vêtements pour en avoir de la place.
The children want to sell some clothes to have more space.

2 Mes parents pourraient recycler des journaux pour en avoir de la place.
My parents could recycle paper in order to have more space.

3 Mon amie voudrait se débarrasser

THE SOUND OF SENTENCES

When you have manipulated sentence elements and played around with transferred patterns, you will still need to give pupils practice in saying sentences aloud. The cadence of any grammar pattern has a musicality of its own and the 'ear' needs to hear it and the 'brain' needs to speak it in order to recognise it. It is also a great aid to recall.

Use the Battleship game format to give them the chance to repeat clauses and phrases over and over again. It works like this:

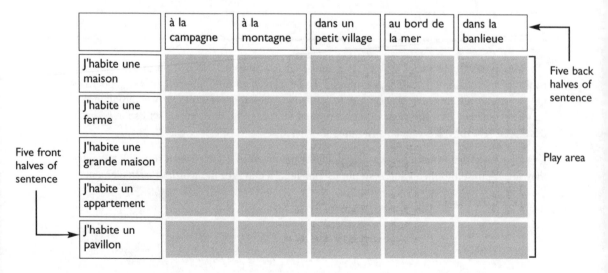

	à la campagne	à la montagne	dans un petit village	au bord de la mer	dans la banlieue
J'habite une maison					
J'habite une ferme					
J'habite une grande maison					
J'habite un appartement					
J'habite un pavillon					

Five front halves of sentence

Five back halves of sentence

Play area

The first halves of the sentences are written down the left-hand side: the second halves are written across the top. Pupils working in pairs must not be able to see the other's sheet: each fills in their own 'ships'– one lot of three squares, two lots of two squares and three lots of one square, in any direction except diagonally.

	à la campagne	à la montagne	dans un petit village	au bord de la mer	dans la banlieue
J'habite une maison	■	■	■		■
J'habite une ferme					
J'habite une grande maison	■			■	
J'habite un appartement	■				
J'habite un pavillon		■			■

Each takes turn to 'fire' a salvo of three shots to try and hit the other's ships. A square is located by its two references, e.g. *J'habite une maison + à la campagne*

A's first go: B's card

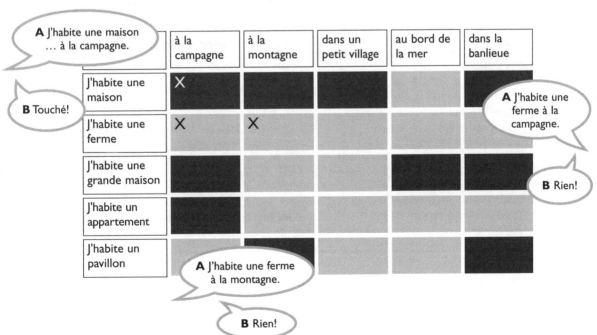

	à la campagne	à la montagne	dans un petit village	au bord de la mer	dans la banlieue
J'habite une maison	X	X	X		
J'habite une ferme	X	X			
J'habite une grande maison					
J'habite un appartement					
J'habite un pavillon					

A J'habite une maison à la montagne.

B Touché!

A J'habite une maison dans un petit village.

B Coulé!

The amount of repetition with variation within a single grammatical pattern that can be achieved in this simple game is quite remarkable. You will need a fund of sentences whose elements are interchangeable.

For example:

Days of the week or time + action
lundi matin + je joue au rugby · *Montag abend + spiele ich Fußball*

(I) live + description of building or place
j'habite + une grande maison · *Ich wohne + in einem Doppelhaus*

Place in the town + direction
la mairie se trouve + à gauche du musée · *das Rathaus ist + neben der Kirche*

Relative clauses
J'ai un ami + qui adore danser · *Ich habe einen Bruder, + der Tiere gern hat*

When using German relative clauses, you will of course have to use all masculine or all feminine or all neuter examples, otherwise it won't work.

Modals
Je peux + jouer ce soir · *Ich muss + meine Hausaufgaben machen*

Past tense
J'ai + regardé · *Ich habe + gesungen*

Word order

This activity is particularly useful in German in order to emphasise word order.

Montag + spiele ich Fußball
Zum Frühstück + esse ich Cornflakes mit Milch und Zucker
Wenn das Wetter schön ist, + gehe ich in die Stadt

All of these exercises in this chapter should either follow or include a large element of reading out loud, chanting patterns aloud and generally reinforcing the look of the words and elements with their sound.

I saw one teacher very effectively using speed and sound to ring the changes of pedestrian repetition. She said the phrases and sentences she had just introduced very quickly or very slowly, very loudly or very softly and the pupils keenly imitated her every change. Sometimes she said things once, sometimes two or three times; sometimes her voice was a mere whisper; on occasions she stamped each word out like a regimental sergeant major. There was no problem getting an active response from those pupils.

Finally take a leaf out of the book of Kellerman and Sharwood Smith (1986), who suggest you 'present the student with English sentences and structures and ask which would:

a transliterate;
b need reordering of syntax;
c need restructuring of concept and therefore words in the target language.'

By reinforcing these three patterns, your pupils will begin to analyse every sentence they meet. And maybe by Year 11 they will be able to come up with an example of all three for a single phrase such as 'I like that':

a *j'aime ça*
b *je l'aime*
c *ça me plaît*

If that sounds light years off, at least take the germ of the idea and get your pupils to analyse into one of the three categories the phrases they are learning each unit. Recall this analysis just before a writing task: list expressions that would be useful under the three headings. It will help remind them that **a** transliteration is not the only option.

10 Dealing with the unknown

In any new language there will be concepts that are quite literally foreign to our way of thinking. And nothing can be stranger than trying to grasp a non-English concept of 'you'. When learning French, English speakers have to first of all understand that 'you' has a singular and a plural application: *'tu'* and *'vous'* and then that it also has a polite application, which covers both singular and plural: *'vous'*. German also asks for the former to be recognised: *'du' and 'ihr'* but uses a third person plural pronoun *'Sie'* for the latter: you polite singular and plural.

It is hard work building up a process of thought that automatically produces the right word for 'you'. Perhaps the explanation given by bilingual and trilingual people about what triggers a language in their brain can help. A friend in Wales was once admonished by our local headteacher for not speaking to me in Welsh in order to help me with the language. She apologised and said, 'I can't. When I look at her, I think in English.' This is apparently a common feeling among bilingual people.

To someone brought up to have more than one way of saying 'you', it is an automatic reaction brought about by whoever they are looking at. For English speakers it requires much thought, training and practice.

Do we simplify matters and just teach *'vous'* and *'Sie'*? A glance through coursebooks will show that this is not the case. We tend to use *'tu'* and *'du'* even though what the pupils will hear most from their teachers is *'vous'* and *'ihr'*. How confusing on the ear, unless the explanation follows. And will words be enough? In this case I am convinced that picturing the varying prompts is the way to engrain this novelty.

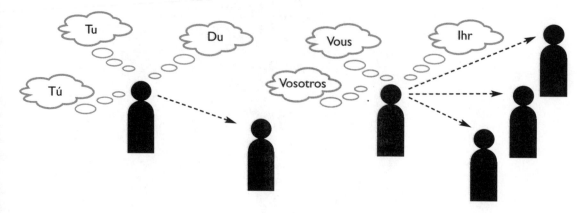

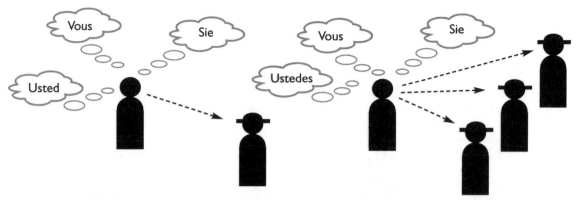

1 Use pictures cut out of magazines to make quick fire prompts. How would you address this person? And this person? And these people? What difference would it make if you addressed this person as '*tu/du/tú*'?

2 Use the facilities of the word processor once more. Insert into a file various clipart images showing one or more people. Next to them insert an Autoshape Callout into which you write all the possible versions of a question with 'you'.

Willst du mitkommen?
Wollt ihr mitkommen?
Wollen Sie mitkommen?

Tu veux une glace?
Vous voulez une glace

¿Quieres beber algo?
¿Queréis beber algo?
¿Quiere beber algo?
¿Quieren beber algo?

Pupils have to:

- decide who is speaking;
- delete the sentence or sentences that aren't appropriate;
- Each callout/speech bubble has a small yellow button at the mouth piece end. Use this to drag the mouthpiece to the person selected.

3 Reinforce in groups by having a tea party! Practise with pictures of the tea things, china, cutlery, sandwiches, cakes, etc. Appoint the players; there must be the two parents (so a child can use the familiar 'you' in the singular and the plural; two guests (who are to be addressed singly and together with the polite form) and two children (who are to be addressed using the familiar form in the singular and the plural). Now let them play! Is it *Passe-moi les biscuits, s.v.p.?* Or *Passez-moi les biscuits, s.v.p.?* Do they ask *Möchtest du eine Tasse Tee?* Or *Möchten Sie eine Tasse Tee?*

4 Assessment: When the groups think they have cracked it, they can then show off to the class – only this time for real! Lay a table with real china and cutlery. Load the large plates with different flavoured sandwiches and cakes or biscuits. Have a real tea pot and milk and

sugar. Each group demonstrating their skills must speak in turn and can stay eating at the table so long as they use a different word for 'you' in every sentence and so long as they make no mistakes. As soon as the first mistake is heard or there is a gap of longer than four seconds without anyone speaking, then they have to 'leave the table'!

5 Practising 'you' should become a constantly repeated starter activity. A quick-fire round of Questions and Answers will help. The teacher calls out the beginnings of a question – enough to reveal the verb: Pupils have to respond orally accordingly, e.g. *Est-ce que tu aimes ...?* Response: *Oui j'aime*, but *Est-ce que vous aimez ...?* Response: *Oui nous aimons ... Tu joues ...? Oui je joue. Vous jouez ...? Oui nous jouons*, etc.

If we are to try to build some level of automaticity into our pupils' production before the end of five years study, this ought to be one of the areas we focus on. Instead of trying to simplify it for them, or confuse them with different patterns without explanation, take the bull by the horns, admit the difficulty, be open about the amount of practice needed and bring on the cream buns as a suitable reward!

▮ WORD ORDER

The strict word order required by German can seem unnecessarily complicated – even just unnecessary. However we do have rules ourselves about the order of words in English – we don't, for example, say 'a red big pencil' nor 'I am going not to town this morning' – so the point needs to be broached not as something utterly unheard of but as something to be expected. It could take many hours of listening and imitating for the brain to deduce what is going on, whereas a simple explanation of what happens, well illustrated with examples from a story or the coursebook, can minimise the strangeness. Then learning a couple of sentence patterns by rote can provide a short cut to learning.

Once again the computer offers active rote learning techniques that will help pupils' understanding. A procedure that involves just three steps can be used to demonstrate inversion, where German changes the word order of simple sentences. The three steps are:

a	Ich spiele jeden Tag Fußball

☐ *Move word/phrase to front of sentence.*

b	jeden Tag Ich spiele Fußball

☐2 *Move subject to position after verb.*

c	jeden Tag spiele Ich Fußball

☐3 *Make changes necessary to capital letters.*

d	Jeden Tag spiele ich Fußball

Turning two short sentences into main and subordinate clause is also easier on the computer! Again a simple three-step procedure must be followed each and every time.

a	Ich gehe nach Hause. Ich bin müde.

1 *Change full stop in sentence 1 to a comma and add* weil/wenn, *etc.*

b	Ich gehe nach Hause, weil Ich bin müde.

2 *Move verb in second sentence to the end in front of the full stop.*

c	Ich gehe nach Hause, weil Ich müde bin.

3 *Make changes necessary to capital letters.*

d	Ich gehe nach Hause, weil ich müde bin.

Exercises like this are hopeless on paper; but on a whiteboard or on a computer screen where words can be literally dragged into new positions, they become simple and straightforward. Demonstrate repeatedly until the pupils can talk **you** through the procedure! Then allow them to work on their own in the ICT room. Once pupils have practised actually moving and changing the sentences, it will not be long before they can translate this into a cognitive procedure, i.e. as a mental process with static writing on a blackboard or on paper. If they seem to forget later on, jog their memories by starting to recite the procedure.

VERBS

The English verb system owes much to the German verb system. Except its novel use of auxiliary + participle or infinitive, it mirrors the German system well.

sing	sings	sang	have sung
singen	*singt*	*sang*	*habe gesungen*
bring	brings	brought	have brought
bringen	*bringt*	*brachte*	*habe gebracht*
make	makes	made	have made
machen	*macht*	*machte*	*habe gemacht*
can	can	could	(have been able to)
können	*kann*	*konnte*	*habe können/gekonnt*

None of the above helps us with French and Spanish verbs and yet there are patterns in common which we could make better use of. By Year 10 pupils should have a good grasp of the parts of the verb and the building of tenses, even if only receptively. To boost productive use, they need to be able to come up with the main changes to the spelling of the root of any irregular verb.

For example, it is common practice in German to learn the parts of the verb if it is an irregular by heart. But it is rare to see this being done in French or Spanish. And yet the root spelling is vital for the construction of tenses. French irregulars divide themselves into two groups.

Group 1:

The infinitive root appears in the present singular: but changes in the present plural.

boire	**bois**	buvons	buvais	bu
écrire	**écris**	écrivons	écrivais	écrit
prendre	**prends**	prenons	prenais	pris

Group 2:

The infinitive root appears in the present plural: but changes in the present singular.

recevoir	reçois	**recevons**	**recevais**	reçu
venir	viens	**venons**	**venais**	venu
savoir	sais	**savons**	**savais**	su

As the imperfect tense will depend on the first person plural root, knowing which category the verb is will help.

I have taught the parts of the verb and a recognition of tenses in German by making cards of:

1 infinitives both regular and irregular;
2 third person singular present;
3 third person singular simple past;
4 past participles.

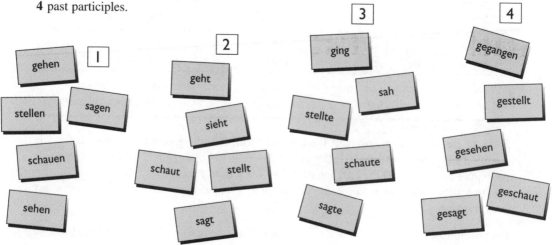

I make sets for about 10–12 verbs. I divide the class into four and hand out the infinitives to the first group, the third person singular present to the next, the third person singular simple past to the next and the past participles to the last group. Then we proceed rather like aural dominoes. I ask a pupil in the 'infinitive' group to call out what is written on a card. I then ask the next group to call out the card they have that is obviously part of that verb: then I do the same with groups three and four. Tentatively to start with, the groups call out *'Schreiben'* *'er ... schreibt?'*, *'Schreib ...* oh no! *schrieb'*, *'err ... geschrieben'*.

We continue in the same way, the pupils getting quicker at spotting the matching verbs and better at the correct pronunciation. After about 4–6 verbs I ask groups three and four if they have begun to notice anything and some bright spark usually points out that there are two patterns: verbs with a *-te* ending or not: past participles with a *-t* or an *-en* ending. I ask if they can hear any connection between the two patterns and ask them to listen while we do the same exercise but in reverse, starting with the past participles. And this time we will also be moving all the cards into two piles – the verbs they hear with *-en* endings in the past participle in one pile and the ones with a *-t* ending in another.

Once we have sorted the cards into two piles in each of the four groups, I ask the infinitive group to take their *-t* ending pile and we reverse and repeat the exercise once more. This time I ask them to listen carefully. After 4–5 verbs I stop and ask the infinitive group to start again with the other pile, again asking them to listen carefully. It usually takes only 2–3 verbs to be completed before someone is putting up their hands and saying 'This lot change their sound/spelling' and I ask for some of the *-t* ending verbs to be run through again. This time they become aware that these do not change their spelling. Very often by this time someone is comparing what they are hearing to English. 'It's like our words. 'Sing, sang, sung' and 'work, worked'. Sometimes they change and sometimes they don't.

I call in all the cards and I start calling out infinitives. I am always surprised by how many pupils are able after such a short time to complete the entire verb. Those pupils with more acute ears than others lead the way, but the rest follow a short distance behind.

As the pupils leave the class, I stand by the door and ask each pupil to finish a verb from the infinitive I give them. With a little prompting from those behind, they all manage to leave the classroom!

A similar activity could work for French and Spanish, For French you would need:

infinitive	first person present singular	first person present plural	first person singular imperfect	the past participle
voir	vois	voyons	voyais	vu
donner	donne	donnons	donnais	donné
écrire	écris	écrivons	écrivais	écrit
finir	finis	finissons	finissais	fini

And for Spanish:

infinitive	first person present singular	first person present plural	first person singular imperfect	the past participle
comer	como	comemos	comía	comido
vivir	vivo	vivimos	vivía	vivido
trabajar	trabajo	trabajamos	trabajaba	trabajado
ir	voy	vamos	iba	ido

The ears would have to work harder to distinguish patterns. Perhaps the regular verbs could be picked out first and then the irregulars subdivided into the two patterns mentioned above.

Verb endings

In Year 7 when verb endings have to be learnt, I add Jigsaws and Straights to the class activities. I have found that pupils are often mystified why verbs should even have so many different endings. By using jigsaws I can talk about endings 'fitting' certain subjects and 'not fitting' others. As they can see the visible proof of this in the jigsaws, they are able to take on the concept much more easily.

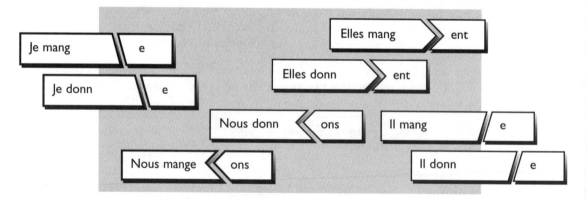

The Straights are sets of cards which have been straight cut rather than 'jigsawed'. Anyone can put the Jigsaw set together, so once pupils think they know the endings, they try the straight set. To find out if they have matched the right ending with the right subject, they then take out the Jigsaw set and piece them together – as these always give the right answer. Jigsaws for practice and answers; Straights for testing yourself.

Reflexive verbs

A couple of years ago I had two English teachers on an MFL INSET. Both had come to see where the common ground was in the KS3 strategy between the two departments. And a discussion on reflexives turned up some interesting differences in attitude.

To them reflexive verbs were not important enough to warrant a particular focus and to this they attributed the fact that, although referred to in the NLS glossary, reflexive verbs do not warrant explanation.

For us in MFL it is hard to consider not treating them as an important grammatical element. For a start they are commonly used in everyday target-language language; most initial French lessons begin with '*Je m'appelle ...*' And yet in contradiction to their common usage, most MFL courses tend to treat them as something difficult, only to be explained in detail to higher level pupils later on. They are most often introduced as a grammar point when daily routines are being covered but are rarely treated explicitly outside of the topic.

Introducing reflexives

a Use the triple translation technique from the start, 'I myself call Lys', 'He himself calls Ben'. This can be left implicit or as another example of a different way of thinking.

b When the topic requires active learning of reflexives, devote time to discussing them in English first of all.

I tell pupils that there are three types of reflexive verbs:

- Obvious reflexives: 'I hit myself. He loves himself. They met each other'.
- Not so obvious reflexives: these have to be thought about. 'I wash. What/who do I wash? I wash myself. I dress. What/who do I dress? I dress myself'.
- And finally unexpected reflexives which are sometimes utterly inexplicable. A good self-explanatory example is 'I am bored' which is reflexive in German, French and Spanish!

    (I bore myself) *sich langweilen*   *s'ennuyer*   *aburrirse*

I show or hand out a list of English words and ask which of the three categories of target-language reflexives do they think they fall into.

| find | wash | look for | hit | walk |
| meet | eat | buy | wake | look at |

The intention is for pupils to discover for themselves that:

a Many verbs can be used reflexively with literal meanings, e.g. 'They hit each other'.
b Many verbs can be used reflexively idiomatically, e.g. 'I found myself wandering down a dark street'.
c Many reflexives don't look reflexive but are reflexive in meaning, e.g. 'I wash, I dress'.
d Some verbs can only be reflexive in the plural, e.g. 'We met under the station clock'.
e Some verbs can only be indirect reflexive, e.g. 'I bought myself ... a pair of shoes. He gave himself a black eye. We stuffed ourselves with hamburgers and chips'.

This kind of work should be followed by an exercise to see how these English ideas translate themselves into the target language by looking them up in dictionaries. What indication does the dictionary give that a verb will be reflexive? Are all English reflexives reflexive in the target language? And vice versa? For these last two exercises, have ready a list of English and target-language reflexives pupils are likely to come across in future topics.

Recognising forms and tenses in reflexives

All the suggestions below for helping pupils practise will aid in the recognition, application and manipulation of reflexives:

- Turn and Learn = matching meaning to target-language form, especially useful for those verbs that are **not** reflexive-looking in English.

- Jigsaws for matching persons + pronouns to verbs or persons + verbs to pronouns.

- Sorting cards into persons.

- Sorting cards into tenses, etc.

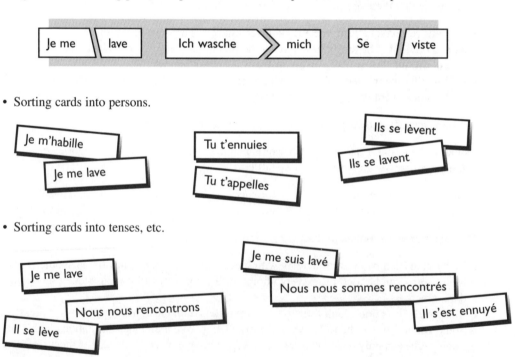

There is nothing inherently more difficult in dealing with reflexives. Once the idea has been firmly lodged in pupils' minds and their eyes become accustomed to recognising the form, once they have practised getting their tongues round the forms, it should only be a matter of time, as with any other verb, before they begin to use them for themselves.

* Conclusion

It is particularly irritating for students of French to observe that tiny children (in France) only just able to form a sentence, normally use the appropriate gender for a noun. In fact, however, students should take courage from this, since it implies the existence of an underlying system. (Surridge:1995)

Surridge continues with sound observation leading to sane advice:

We may take comfort from the fact that small children use much less vocabulary than we do – and then suddenly we realise that we have stumbled on part of their secret: children learn one stratum of vocabulary thoroughly, complete with noun genders, before preceding to the next.

If we were to follow this advice and cover fewer topics more thoroughly, focussing earlier more on grammar and form, with less breadth, but greater depth, perhaps our pupils would be able to build up a better system for themselves. At the moment we still feed them piecemeal such disparate chunks of language that maybe they never get the opportunity to take in enough in order to see patterns. It will take a monumental change of direction in foreign language teaching before suggestions such as Surridge's can be implemented. Perhaps primary languages can take it on? Making sure that pupils arrive in secondary school with fewer topics covered, less breadth of vocabulary but instead a sound understanding of gender and agreement, a verb system beyond the present and an expectation of the transferability of elements within a sentence.

In the meantime, restricted as we are by the dictates of the exam syllabus and our coursebook, what can we do to ensure effective learning? Make it active! Make it visual! Make it vivid! Make it meaningful! But above all do it over and over again! It is the repetition that will lay down the neural pathways, that will one day allow the automatic response to surprise, not just you, but the pupil as well.

We should not consider extended practice a waste of time. We should be taking as much time as the pupils in front of us need. For some it will take a longer, for others a shorter time. But if we do not ensure comprehension of concept, sound learning techniques, adequate time to evolve a good recall system, then we should not be surprised, when the initial fervour of the pupils runs out of steam – somewhere around National Curriculum Level 4.

Suddenly the next steps along the continuum of learning appear insurmountable – as in truth they are for many. All buildings need foundations; if care is taken to build solid foundations, then the brick walls take no time at all to be erected. But if the walls are built directly onto the ground, then the weight of a few courses of bricks will cause the whole building to sink into the mud.

If our pupils are to get beyond the first few levels of the MFL National Curriculum they will need to have a better understanding of language, more time to accustom their eyes and ears to the sounds and the look of the new language and have to spend more time in preparation before the end result – performing in the target language.

Rather than dictating the pace of learning in the early years, we should be ensuring that the individual needs of our pupils are being addressed. If they can't do something, it could be, because:

• we are asking them to do it too soon;
• we have not given them enough time to absorb the new work;
• we have not helped them find an effective way of learning;
• we haven't taken into account their own hypotheses on language and language learning or uncovered any possible misconceptions;
• we haven't asked them where the problem lies.

Unless we analyse the mistakes they are making, we will not know which particular hurdles they are facing at any one time.

If we don't probe their learning styles and ask them to share the problems and difficulties they may be having, they may be developing silently all sorts of hypotheses which may in the end prevent any real progress.

And if we make light of the task they are facing, instead of pointing out that initially it is going to be a long slow haul – but one which in the long run they are all capable of – they may become discouraged at their seeming lack of progress after all the effort they are putting in.

One thing we can assure them – anyone can speak a second language … or a third or a fourth. **The human brain is well adapted to be a polyglot.** It is just that they are not learning it under ideal conditions. With on average only two hours of lessons per week over five years, the time spent learning by the average pupil is the equivalent of spending fifteen days in the country concerned! So relatively they do make excellent progress, in fact a great deal more than they would do if they visited the country for just over a fortnight. So comparatively, for the time spent, their effort really is worthwhile. But they need to be told this.

Let us leave the last word to Lauren. With reference to teaching the ears to see and the eyes to hear, at nearly five, Lauren tells her mother about new words she's learnt 'I've got it in my eyes now, Mummy' (Barnes 2004).

So she has and let us hope for our pupils' sakes, they get the target language in their eyes too!

References

Ackermann, D. (1996) *A natural history of the senses.* Phoenix/Orion.

Barnes, A. (2004) *Private communication.*

Beeching, K. (1989) *Grammar is dead! Long live system-building!* BALT 27 (2).

Biriotti, L. (1999) Young Pathfinder 8: *Grammar is fun.* CILT.

Bodmer, F. (1944; reprinted 1987) *The loom of language.* Merlin.

Brumfit, C. (1980) 'From defining to designing communicative methodology in foreign language teaching'. *Studies in Language Acquisition* 3.1: 1–9.

Bullock, A. (1975) *A language for life: the Bullock report.* HMSO.

Channel 4 and Green Umbrella Ltd and QWGBH Boston (1995) *The mystery of the senses: sight* (see also Ackermann above).

Clark, as quoted in Wode (1974): 'Developmental sequence: an alternative approach to morpheme order' in *Language Learning,* Vol 28.

Cook, V. J. (1982) 'Second language learning: a psycholinguistic perspective'. In: Kinsella, V. (ed) *Surveys 1.* Cambridge University Press.

Cox (1989): *The Cox report.* HMSO.

DfEE (1990) *Modern foreign languages for ages 11–16.* DfEE.

Edelman, G. (1987) *Neural Darwinism.* Penguin.

Greenfield, S. (1997) *The human brain, a guided tour.* Weidenfeld and Nicolson.

Hawkins, E. (1987) *Awareness of language: an introduction.* Cambridge University Press.

Hawkins, E. (1981) *Modern languages in the curriculum.* Cambridge University Press.

Hewer, S. (1996) 'Information technology'. In: Hawkins, E. (ed) *Thirty years of language teaching.* CILT.

Kellerman, E. and Sharwood Smith, M. (1986) *Crosslinguistic influence in second language acquisition.* Oxford.

Kingman (1988) Teaching of English language: *The Kingman report*. HMSO.

Manning, P. 'Computers, learners and teaching strategies'. In: *EUROCALL 1991* (Helsinki).

MFL National Curriculum Working Party (1992) *Modern Foreign Languages for ages 11–16:* 56, 9.18. DfEE.

Pillette, M. (1997) *Camarades 2*. Nelson Thornes.

Rendall, H. (2006) *Just Click. Na klar! 1* ICT Resource. Nelson Thornes.

Rigault, A. (1971) *La grammaire du français parlé*. Paris: Hachette.

Ringbom, H. (1987) *The role of the first language in the foreign language learning classroom*. Multilingual Matters.

Ringbom, H. (1986) 'Crosslinguistic influence and the foreign language learning process'. In: Kellerman, E. and Sharwood Smith, M. *Cross-linguistic influence in second language acquisition*. Pergamon.

Surridge, M. (1995) *Le ou la? The gender of French nouns*. Multilingual Matters.

Walls, D. (1992) 'Survival or fluency?'. In: *ReCALL* 7.

Wilson (1999) Lingu@NET Forum message.

Winkley, Sir D. *'Grey matters': Current neurological research and its implications for educators' TES*/Keele seminar 1999.

Further reading

Christiansen, M. H. and Kirby, S. (2004) *Language evolution*. Oxford University Press.

Edelman, G. (1992) *Bright air, brilliant fire*. Penguin.

Rendall, H. (2001) 'Developing a sense of gender in French' in Atkinson, T. (ed) Reflections on Practice 7: *Reflections on ICT*. CILT.

Sacks, O. (1989) *Seeing voices*. Picador.

See also **www.ict4lt.org** for ICT for foreign language teaching.